Lifesong

Bible-centered worship for the Emerging Generation

Oliver Claassen

CHRISTIAN
FOCUS

Copyright © Oliver Claassen 2008

ISBN 978-1-84550-373-4

Published in 2008 by
Christian Focus Publications, Geanies House,
Fearn, Ross-shire, IV20 1TW, Scotland

www.christianfocus.com

Cover design by www.moose77.com

Printed and bound in Denmark by Norhaven

To contextualize God's Word lovingly without compromising its truth requires great skill and a gospel heart. Dr. Oliver Claassen has both, as evidenced in his new book, "Lifesong – bible centered worship for the emerging generation." Though written with high school and college students in mind, Dr. Claassen helps a much larger audience understand the difference between worshipping worship and worshipping God. Both the style and content of this book reflect the heart of a man passionate about God's glory, and pastorally committed to leading God's people into a more faithful and engaging experience of God's worship in line with the truth of the gospel.

Scotty Smith
Founding Pastor, Christ Community Church,
Franklin, TN

Lifesong is part of a movement of God's spirit that is leading emerging generations to return to Christ centered worship that values beauty and artistry. I applaud the creativity of these melodies and their ability to lead us back to singing the scriptures to one another.

Chris Seay
Pastor of Ecclesia Houston
President of Ecclesia Bible Society

Outstanding! Oliver brings clarity to one of the most misunderstood subjects of my 20 years in student ministry. He looks at what the Bible actually says about God's desire for and from His worshippers. This is written for those of us who want more than a superficial discussion of what worship is and is not; but without the lingo only theologians can understand. All over the country I am asked about worship, now I will point them to this book. Thanks Oliver.

David McNeely, Speaker
Senior High Campus Director at Perimeter Church
Atlanta, GA

The great value of this work on worship is its rooting in Scripture, its powerful and sustained focus on the glorious person and work of Christ, and the demonstration of the relevance of worship to all of life. Worship is not reduced to the level of technique or one time-honored cultural expression or a heartless, outward duty. Africa with its traditional view of a distant God and mediatory ancestral cult needs this work that so powerfully links the worshipper directly with the transcendent God through the revelatory, atoning, reconciling, intercessory and reigning ministries of the Lord Jesus Christ. This doctrine-packed book is also good news for Africa because it understands the necessary cultural dimension of true and fervent worship, and therefore champions a place for an African form of worship that resonates so much with the worship taught and exemplified in the Bible, especially the Old Testament. May the Lord be pleased to use this book in His worldwide church to recapture the heart and dynamic of a God-centered worship where God's redeemed creatures glory in His worthship and every sphere of life pulsates with worship.

Vernon Light, Principal
The Bible Institute of the Eastern Cape
Port Elizabeth, South Africa.

Lifesong is a good introduction to biblical worship for our teachning. We will use it to train students that true worship is biblical worship that responds to God's revelation in the bible. Pastor Oliver has given us good material for the equipping of Pastors in teaching their people aobut the worship of God with all of life.

Reuben Sitati, President
Webuye Ministry Training Institute
Kenya

Contents

Acknowledgements

As followers of the Lord Jesus Christ we stand upon the shoulders of His servants who have gone before us. I thank God for their teachings that have helped shape my understanding of Scripture. Some are mentioned in the endnotes, but many whose insights reflected and used in this book are not. I hope I have not offended anyone for failing to give due credit for their ideas or publications. I particularly want to thank the congregation at EPC for their love of God's word and encouragement to the ministerial team at EPC who have seen this project as a worthwhile,Christ honoring project. I thank Lee Johnson, Louisa Burton, Sam Rowen, Matt Bennett and David Rogers. Andrew Claassen's passion, commitment and contribution to music in worship is infectious. His arrangements of the Psalms have enahanced our worship. All have spurred me on to complete this project. I thank Martin Maclean and the folk at Christian Focus for their support.

***Together Everyone Accomplished More
(T.E.A.M.)
To God Be the Glory!***

Dr Oliver Claassen after a career in education in South Africa and Scotland studied at Covenant Seminary, St Louis and Westminster, Philadelphia. Serving with *Mission to the World* (*MTW*) he planted churches in Australia before serving as Far East Director for *MTW*. His ministry experience includes serving as Senior Pastor of Westminster PCA in Atlanta, Missions Pastor at Twin Oaks PCA in St Louis and his present charge in Cape Coral, Florda (www.epchurch.net). Oliver is married to Helen and they have five children – Daniel, David, Anna-Grace, Andrew and Phillip.'

Chapter One

What is this thing called Worship?

Worship is declaring, with our lips and lives, that God is more important than anything else to us, that he is our deepest desire, and that his inherent worth is beyond everything else we hold dear.

In the revelation of Jesus Christ, which God gave John on the island of Patmos, the unique worth of God is heralded in songs of praise.

> … behold, a throne stood in heaven, with one seated on the throne. (3) And he who sat there had the appearance of jasper and carnelian, and around the throne was a rainbow that had the appearance of an emerald.(4) Around the throne were twenty-four thrones, and seated on the thrones were twenty-four elders, clothed in white garments, with golden crowns on their heads…(6b) And around the throne,

> *on each side of the throne, are four living creatures…*
> *(8b) and day and night they never cease to say, Holy,*
> *holy, holy, is the Lord God Almighty, who was and*
> *is and is to come!… (10) the twenty-four elders fall*
> *down before him who is seated on the throne and*
> *worship him who lives for ever and ever. They cast*
> *their crowns before the throne, saying, (11) Worthy*
> *are you, our Lord and God, to receive glory and honor*
> *and power, for you created all things, and by your will*
> *they existed and were created.*
>
> *(Rev. 4:2-11 ESV)*

God alone is worthy of worship, for He alone is inherently righteous. The Psalmists declare this truth in their songs of worship.

> *Righteous are you, O LORD, and right are your rules.*
> *(Ps. 119:137 ESV)*

> *Enter not into judgment with your servant, for no one*
> *living is righteous before you.*
> *(Ps. 143:2 ESV)*

> *Righteousness and justice are the foundation of your*
> *throne; steadfast love and faithfulness go before*
> *you.*
> *(Ps. 89:14 ESV)*

Louie Giglio points out that worship is simply about value. Our worship is a response to what we value most. It is easy to identify what we value most by the things we do. We consider that a person, a thing, or an experience is what matters most. This consideration can be in the form of a position, a status, a job, or something we own. We are willing to sacrifice in order to achieve that which has become of ultimate value. Worship is coming before the "throne" of what is of ultimate value to us. We are willing to sacrifice in order to grab hold of what is of ultimate value to us. In the Old Testament the priests would build an altar on which to offer the sacrifices to the One whom they worshipped. In the New Testament the priestly sacrifice is described as *"Through him (Jesus) then let us continually offer up a sacrifice of praise to God, that is, the fruit of lips that acknowledge his name. Do not neglect to do good and to share what you have, for such sacrifices are pleasing to God"* (Heb 13:15-16).

Everyone who is willing to sacrifice has first to build an altar.[1] In order to find your altar of worship just follow the trail of how you use your time, energy, money, affections. To whom or what do you offer your allegiance? At the end of the trail you will find what it is that you worship. The more time you spend before that throne the more your life will reflect what or whom you worship. It is abundantly clear that our actions speak louder than words.

Test your actions to see what it is you really worship. Don't be surprised if you discover that God is not the object of your worship. Jesus Himself warns us by saying, *"Not everyone who says (words) to me 'Lord, Lord,' will enter the kingdom of heaven, but he who does (actions) the will of my Father who is in heaven"* (Matt. 7:21).

13

Humankind is made to worship

The Scriptures teach us that we are creatures made in the image of God with a very specific mandate to be a communing co-laborer with God in the rule of His world. The very essence of being human is to seek to fulfill this command of God in relationship with Him. In doing so we shape our world as culture-building creatures who often forget that we are first of all subjects of a Kingdom that is not of this world.

Since worship is rooted in our image-bearing DNA, what we worship 'inwardly' will be reflected 'outwardly'. The result of this dynamic is that the object of our worship will be seen as either the Creator Righteous God or the cultural objects we make in our image.

The purpose and action in worship must not to be confused with personal feelings – effects or by-products of worship. Worship can occur without ecstatic or emotional feelings. You do not worship in order to "experience worship" or to have some kind of emotional experience. The act of worship occurs when God is honored and given the worth that is His due. In worship you do not come to get. You come to worship in order to give. You come to meet with God and to give Him the glory due his name.

Our goal in worship is to engage God, to come into His presence, to call to mind that He is with us, to glorify and enjoy Him, to commune with Him and receive His favor. In biblical worship we focus upon God Himself.[2]

The Manner of worship

Worship comes in many different forms because the church of Jesus Christ comes to us in many different forms. One only has to look at the history of the expansion of the church to see that the forms of the church are as diverse as the cultures in which they exist. God is not contained in a box nor bound to manifest His presence in every place in the same form. God's grace has many different cultural expressions (1 Pet. 4:10). Though the bible clearly shows that there are universal principles that govern the form of worship it is significant to note that there is diversity in the specific cultural expression in the worship of God. The meaning of worship is not faceless. There are certain dimensions that are present wherever there is the true worship of God. The manner in which these dimensions are expressed are culturally diverse.

Continuing Principles of Worship

The words of Jesus in His interaction with the Samaritan woman in John chapter 4 give some instruction about true worship. They sat together by a well at the base of mountains Gerizim and Ebal. The mountains were significant in the life of Israel. After the children of Israel were delivered from Egyptian bondage, they wandered through the wilderness for forty years. After entering the land promised to them by God they had a great ceremony in which they renewed their covenant vows to God. The tribes of Israel were divided and half went up on

Mount Gerizim and half of the tribes went up on Mount Ebal. There they cried out across the valley the blessings and the curses of the covenant.

The Samaritans were a mixed race of people who were partly Jewish; yet, the Jews despised the Samaritans. The Samaritans continued certain dimensions of the worship of Israel because it was part of their history. They built an altar on Mount Gerizim and offered sacrifices to God. With Mount Gerizim in full view, the woman asked Jesus about the true place of worship

There was a difference between Jews and Samaritans. She says, *(20) "Our fathers worshiped on this mountain, but you say that in Jerusalem is the place where people ought to worship." "This mountain"* is Mt Gerizim which overlooks Jacob's well near Nablus. The Samaritans had their own temple there until it was destroyed by the Jewish King Hyrcanus in 129 B.C. The Samaritans confined Scripture to the Pentateuch so they had no loyalty to the rest of the O.T. and the teachings from God to David about building a temple in Jerusalem. They understood from Deuteronomy that Mt Gerizim was the place that the blessings were to be shouted to God's covenant community (Deut. 27:2-7, 12). The Samaritan woman engages Jesus into this theological debate and Jesus answers, *(21) "Woman, believe me, the hour is coming when neither on this mountain nor in Jerusalem will you worship the Father. (22) You worship what you do not know; we worship what we know, for salvation is from the Jews. (23) But the hour is coming, and is now here, when the true worshipers will worship the Father in spirit and truth, for the Father is seeking such people to worship him. (24) God is spirit, and those who worship him must worship in spirit and truth."* Jesus is not drawn into the debate, He says that the Jews are right because of the stream of revelation they have from God in the Jewish Scriptures. The Jews were to make God's truth known to all people, *salvation is from the Jews.* The point of where to worship is no longer relevant because a new way of worship is taking the place of a physical temple or holy site. It is not the place that matters, but that God is worshiped.

When we come to grasp the meaning of Jesus' words about the kind of people God is seeking to worship Him, then we will be able to understand the manner of worship which is acceptable to God. The words *"in spirit and truth"* direct us to appreciate both the universal principles of worship and the different forms of worship experienced among God's people in His culturally mosaic world.

The Act of Worship

When Jesus was born, wealthy men from the East traveled a long distance to find Him. They exemplified a foundational truth about worship, namely *worship is from the heart to God through Christ our Savior.*

These wise men have become the most celebrated worshipers of all time, yet when they found Jesus, there were no songs and no speeches, at least none that are recorded. Matthew 2:11 simply says that when they saw Him, they *'fell down and worshiped Him.'* Their reaction was immediate and passionate and totally without any musical lead-in that would have put them in the mood for a holy moment. Worship happened at the instant these men recognized Jesus for who He is, and that revelation was so powerful, they could not stay on their feet."[3]

Worship from the heart can be difficult in corporate worship. It is very different in form from that of the Magi's worship experience. The reason for the difference is that we draw the principles of corporate worship from all of Scripture—God's truth—not one experience only.

Once we understand what God in Scripture actually commands for worship, we will see that God leaves a number of things to our discretion and allows considerable flexibility in the application of His principles within different cultural contexts.

Different cultures have different styles of applying God's eternal commands with respect to worship. This difference in cultural methodology can lead to division within a mono-cultural congregation of believers familiar with only one tradition of worship practice. In the Book of Acts, for example, we read how Christian worship practice clashed with the traditions of the Jewish temple practice. Later, English Puritans excluded symbolism and religious holidays with the exception of the Sabbath in their worship practice. The Puritan method was an example of one cultural application for corporate worship for Christians.

Neither their cultural practice nor any other cultural practice should be made a universally binding biblical mandate for the manner of worship.

A congregation's practice of worship not only reflects some of the cultural practices of its worshipers but also reflects preferences emerging from the historic context in which the local congregation emerged. Understanding this concept of "univer-sal principles-of-Scripture-applied-variously" helps clarify our understanding of the cross-cultural application of the Scriptural principles of worship.

No one cultural tradition is static; cultures are dynamic and changing. While biblical principles never change, methodology and expression of worship principles will always reflect some of the cultural context and its changes. This makes for various styles in worship practice but aids worship from the heart through Christ.

In Scripture there are two groups of Hebrew and Greek terms that are translated "worship." The first group refers to "labor" or "service." These terms refer historically to the service of God carried out by the priests in the tabernacle and the temple during the Old Testament period. The second group of terms means literally "bowing" or "bending the knee," hence, "paying homage, honoring the worth of someone else," as the Magi did before the infant Christ.[4] The English term *worship*, derived from *worthship*, has the same connotation. From the usage of these terms, we may conclude that worship is an active experience. It is something we do. Worship is a verb[5]. In worship we are not to be passive but to work at participating in the honoring of God our Savior through our adoration and service.

As recorded in the *Acts of the Apostles,* soon after Christ's resurrection and ascension the early church transitioned from a Jewish cultural form of worship to include the worship of Christ. An early example of worship is in Acts 4:23-31. After suffering persecution for honoring Him, the disciples actively worshiped in praise and in prayer directed by Scripture.

These Christians wished to proclaim the truth of Jesus, *"Immanuel",* which translated means "God with us" (Matt. 1:23), so they acknowledged God and worshiped Him for His presence with them. Acts 4:24 says, *"They raised their voices together in prayer to God."* Their prayer acknowledged God's will and greatness. *"Sovereign Lord,"* they said, *"you made the heaven and the earth and the sea, and everything in them."* They recognized and thanked God for communing with them through the Old Testament recorded word of prophecy of Psalm 2.

In Acts 4:24-26 the disciples *"raised their voices together in prayer to God...You spoke by the Holy Spirit through the mouth of your servant, our father David: 'Why do the nations rage and the peoples plot in vain? The kings of the earth take their stand and the rulers gather together against the Lord and against his Anointed One.'"*

They comforted themselves with the knowledge that God had shown His trustworthiness in keeping

His word in fulfilling that particular prophecy in the events of the Crucifixion of Jesus.

They actively worshiped Christ Jesus as Lord of all, honoring Him as the worthy Savior of His people from their sins.

An account from French history illustrates God's worthiness in worship. In 1715, Louis XIV of France died. Louis, who called himself "the Great", was the monarch who made the infamous statement, "I am the State!" His court was the most magnificent in Europe, and his funeral was spectacular. His body lay in a golden coffin. To dramatize the deceased king's greatness, orders had been given that the cathedral would be very dimly lit with only one special candle set above his coffin. Thousands waited in hushed silence. Then Bishop Massilon began to speak. Slowly reaching down, he snuffed out the candle, saying, "Only God is great!"

We honor God with our worship as we offer Him our praise from the heart through Christ. Only God is worthy of worship.

Deducing Principles of Worship from the biblical record

What principles of worship can we deduce from this record? They were standing in awe of God's mighty acts, hearing His authoritative word, and fellowshipping with Him in prayer. They worked joyfully in recognition of the Lord's presence. God was really among them. Acts 4:31 reads: "*After they prayed, the place where they were meeting was shaken.*

And they were all filled with the Holy Spirit and spoke the word of God boldly." They called on the Lord, the Anointed One, the Sovereign Lord, the holy Savior Jesus, through whom God heals and performs miraculous signs and wonders. They proclaimed the power and majesty of Christ and the word of God. This was later to become an expected principle evidenced in corporate worship as the Apostle Paul directs in his letters to the Corinthian church. 1 Corinthians 14:24-25 reads: *"But if an unbeliever or someone who does not understand comes in while everybody is prophesying, he will be convinced by all that he is a sinner and will be judged by all, and the secrets of his heart will be laid bare, so he will fall down and worship God, exclaiming, 'God is really among you!'"* Prophecy, namely teaching and expounding God's Scripture, leads unbelievers to worship God as the Holy Spirit convicts them of God's presence in their midst through the preaching of God's word.

Christ Jesus is so central in the disciples' thinking and speaking that they give a Christ-centered, biblically-based testimony to His presence with them. Their personal experience with the Lord is so real that they see affliction and resistance to their testimony of Christ's rule as a confirmation of God's rule and power spoken through the prophets of old. They acknowledge God's revealed will in their corporate worship practice. They remember Scripture. They pray.

The disciples' love and trust in the Lord springs up like a fountain in their prayer to God. Acts 4:24 states,

"They raised their voices together in prayer to God." Culturally different applications of this principle of the practice of prayer in worship are seen in the way Koreans, Latin American Columbians and global Pentecostal assemblies encourage the assembled people to pray aloud at the same time. Some Scottish Presbyterian assemblies all sing or read a Psalm in unison, or recite The Lord's Prayer together, but they would not ordinarily pray individual prayers aloud at the same time. What is important is not the method of application of this principle of prayer in worship as much as the oneness in mind and purpose in prayer. The disciples' prayer was that God would enable them to proclaim Christ as Lord and Redeemer of sinners and healer of the sick.[6]

The form of prayer may differ from culture to culture but the common prayer book of the church universal is surely the Book of Psalms. In the apostolic worship service of Acts 4, Psalm 2 is their prayer. This action by the apostles has become a principle of corporate worship in the church universal. The abiding principle of prayer as an act of worship is found in its definition as given in the Westminster Shorter Catechism,

> *Prayer is the offering up our desires unto God for things agreeable to His will, in the name of Christ, with confession of our sins, and thankful acknowledgment of his mercies.*[7]

The Corporate Worship Experience

Could it be that we do not experience the power of God in our worship because we are neither as dependent on the Holy Spirit nor as aware of Christ's presence as the disciples were in their corporate times of worship? Are we more focused on the style of music or actions of other worshipers than on Christ? Are we neglecting the reading and teaching of Scripture? The disciples were filled with the Spirit because they were filled with Spirit-given Scripture, God's ultimate authority, the very word of God without error.

When Christians gather together to worship, Jesus Christ is with them. (Matt. 18:20) Christ has redeemed them. Christ, crucified, dead, and risen, is the One who heals sinners and makes them whole.

The disciples worshiped God. They had seen God in Christ, sovereign in His rule, faithful to His word, overwhelming in His love and compassion, zealous in accomplishing God the Father's will. Their worship encounter with the resurrected Savior is aptly summarized in the words of William Temple, "To worship is to quicken the conscience by the holiness of God, to feed the mind with the truth of God, to purge the imagination by the beauty of God, to open the heart to the love of God, to devote the will to the purpose of God."[8] True worship is the action of being quickened, fed, purged, and open to Christ the Lord, and deepened devotionally by the Spirit of God (see Luke 11:13). It is to honor Him with words and psalms, hymns and spiritual songs of praise.

More often than not, praise and prayer are in the singing of Psalms.[9] Worship in the tradition of the Old Testament songwriters is still culturally relevant today. The Old Testament songwriters put their words of praise into song with the use of melodies peculiar to their culture accompanied by instruments that now may seem strange to us. They prayed to God in song and so did the New Testament disciples in their context that exhorts us to sing from the heart with words true to Scripture and to use culturally acceptable instruments. Psalm 150 states this universal principle of worship in music as,

> [1]*Praise the Lord,*
> *Praise God in his sanctuary;*
> *praise him in his mighty heavens.*
> [2]*Praise him for his acts of power;*
> *Praise him for his surpassing greatness.*
> [3]*Praise him with the sounding of the trumpet,*
> *praise him with the harp and lyre,*
> [4]*praise him with tambourine and dancing,*
> *Praise him with strings and flute,*
> [5]*praise him with the clash of cymbals,*
> *Praise him with the resounding cymbals.*
> [6]*Let everything that has breath praise the Lord.*
> *Praise the Lord.*

Chapter Two

Who should we Worship?

You go to Sunday worship, but you feel out of sorts. The opening hymn seems wordy and meaningless. You wonder, "Why am I here? Perhaps this worship thing is just a projection of your mind. God is different to different people isn't he? Where does the idea of God come from anyway? How do we know that he is infinite and holy?" Perhaps you feel a little guilty about these thoughts and wish you could get rid of them.

Admitting our doubts and critical thinking before God is a prerequisite for God's Spirit to do His work in us. We need to be honest with Him and acknowledge our unbelief. *"If we confess our sins, he is faithful and just and will forgive us our sins and purify us from all unrighteousness,"* says the Apostle John (1 John 1: 9).

Our ancestors in the faith had a healthy sense of their inadequacies before the great and holy God. Even the Psalmist has to exhort us all to "Praise Him all creatures here below!" All our questions about God have answers that humble us causing us to confess that God is supreme and holy and we are not. The answers to our questions about God are found in His revealed word, the recorded writings of the biblical writers, through whom God spoke to humanity.

God is Knowable

God has made Himself known in appearing to the very human creatures He has made. His act of revealing Himself was first to *"our forefathers through the prophets at many times and in various ways"* and finally, in *"His Son"* (Heb. 1:1-3). Jesus of Nazareth is the true source of our knowledge of God. Jesus affirms that God made Himself known in words and deeds as recorded in the Scriptures. Two such places are Psalm 145 and Acts 17:22-31. There we learn that since God is the all-powerful Creator and Sustainer of everything, He alone is to be worshipped.

> *Great is the Lord and most worthy of praise; His greatness no one can fathom.*
>
> *(Ps.145: 3)*

> *And He is not served by human hands, as if He needed anything, because He himself gives all men life and breath and everything else.*
>
> *(Acts 17:25)*

28

The Lord is righteous in all His ways and loving toward all He has made and fulfills the desire of those who fear Him.

(Ps. 145:17, 19)

Great is the Lord.

(Ps. 145:3)

The God we worship not only created us but He rules over us. Paul addressed the Athenians in Acts 17:23-24:

Men of Athens! I see that in every way you are very religious. For as I walked around and looked carefully at your objects of worship, I even found an altar with this inscription: TO AN UNKNOWN GOD. Now what you worship as something unknown I am going to proclaim to you. The God who made the world and everything in it is the Lord of heaven and earth and does not live in temples built by hands. And he is not served by human hands, as if he needed anything.

God does not depend on His creatures; His creatures depend on him. King David recognized this fact in Psalm 118:28 when he wrote, *"You are my God, and I will exalt you."*

One of the primary ways to get to know God is in His self disclosure to us in Scripture. We learn who He is in the names He gives to Himself. His name reflects the nature and the character of who He is.

We encounter the first name for God in the first verse of Genesis. *"In the beginning God created the heavens and the earth."* Here the word God is the translation of the Hebrew *Elohim*. The name *Elohim* means Creator God. It is a plural noun, but does not mean that there is more than one God.[10] The word is used to describe the diversity and richness in God's Being. He is the King who rules over the universe and His creatures tell of the glory of His kingdom and speak of His might. God's kingdom is everlasting and His dominion endures through all generations (Ps. 145:11, 13). God's rule never ceases at any point in time.

Before anything ever existed, God has existed always. He is the Lord who revealed Himself to Moses as *Yahweh* "I Am Who I Am", the eternal, self-sustaining, self-existing all glorious Creator God (Exo. 3:14). He is the God of grace, truth, goodness, mercy, justice, power, knowledge, and eternality. One word summarizes these attributes – 'glory'. The glory of God is intrinsic to His nature; glory belongs in His essential Being.

Beware, there are false gods

In contrast, man's glory is granted to him by God. If you have a king, remove his robe and crown, give him only rags to wear, leave him on the streets for a few weeks, then put him next to a beggar and you will never know who is who. The only glory a king has is what is given him: a crown, a robe, and a throne. He has no glory originating from within himself. God's glory is intrinsic to His Being. In Acts 17:29 Paul reminds us, *"We should not think that the Divine Being is like gold or silver or stone—an image made by man's design and skill."* If we did think this way then we would be making God out of the imagination of our minds. But our being and our existence derive from God and depend on him. Therefore we ought to worship Him, our Creator, and not the idols of our minds or hands. To worship anything other than God is idolatry.

John Stott writes,

> 'Idolatry is the attempt either to localize God confining him within limits which we impose, whereas He is the Creator of the universe; or to domesticate God, making him dependent on us, taming and taping him, whereas he is the Sustainer of human life; or to alienate God, blaming him for his distance and his silence, whereas he is the Ruler of nations, and not far from any of us; or to dethrone God, demoting him to some image of our own contrivance or craft, whereas he is our Father from whom we derive our being. In brief, all idolatry tries to minimize the gulf between the Creator and his creatures, in order to bring him under our control. More than that, it actually reverses the respective positions of God and us, so that, instead of our humbly acknowledging that God has created and rules us, we presume to imagine that we can create and rule God.'[11]

Turn to God from false gods

Paul in his address to the Athenians points out that God created men so that they would seek Him and perhaps reach out for God and find Him, though He is not far from each one of us. This hope is unfulfilled because of human sin, as the rest of Scripture makes clear. Sin alienates people from God. But even in their alienation they grope for Him. Stott points out that it would be absurd, however, to blame God for this alienation or to regard Him as distant, unknowable, and uninterested. *"He is not far from each one of us" (Acts17:27)*. It is we who are far from Him. If it were not for sin that separates us from God, He would be readily accessible to us. *"For in Him we live and move and have our being"* (Acts 17:28). God made us for Himself.

God made us to worship and enjoy Him. Listen to David's statements in Psalm 145:8-9. *"The Lord is gracious and compassionate; slow to anger and rich in love. The Lord is good to all; He has compassion on all He has made."* God is a loving God and His love cannot change. His compassion never fails even in the midst of affliction and doubt and guilt feelings. He disciplines those whom He loves in order to bring them to experience His mercy and forgiveness (See Prov. 3:11-12). Paul tells us that God is the judge of all the earth (Acts 17:31). God is reliable, faithful, just, and loving.

God forgives and receives sinners

God's dealing with Adam and Eve after their rebellion against His rule helps us understand His just but loving nature. After Adam,[12] the representative of mankind, disobeyed God because of the desire to rule himself rather than worship his creator, it was God who called Adam to return. God had every right to wipe Adam from the face of the earth, because He is Creator King and His subjects are to obey Him. God spared Adam from judgment by promising a male child to come from the woman – a redeemer who would crush the serpent's head (Gen. 3:15), and suffer in that act of deliverance by having his heel bruised.

In the fullness of time the Son of Adam's lineage was born to the Virgin Mary, conceived by the power of the Holy Spirit. The eternal Son of God became man (Phil. 2:6-8). The God-man Jesus, the second Adam (1 Cor. 15:45), kept God's laws. Punishment for Adam's sin was meted out on Jesus by way of the cross. Those who call on the Lord for mercy can escape God's justice and promise of destruction (Ps. 145:18, 20) just as Adam and Eve did in believing God's promise and received God's forgiveness. Though God is just He is also merciful. God gave them the ability to believe His promise and they were restored to a right relationship with God. God satisfied His justice on the male child who suffered in the place of sinners (See Isaiah 53:3-11; Galatians 3:26).

If we are to worship God with a clear conscience, we too must believe God's promise of forgiveness through trusting His Redeemer, the Lord Jesus Christ. We approach God in worship by first admitting our need of His mercy. We confess our sins in prayer in a manner similar to this "I have fallen. I have strayed from your ways like a lost sheep. I have followed the devices of my own heart. I have done those things that I ought not to have done. There is no health in me. But, you, O Lord, are merciful. Be compassionate to me. Restore me. I am sorry for my sin, Lord. Since you are near to all who call on you, to all who call on you in truth, I turn to you. Lord, I fear your name. Hear my cry and deliver me."[13]

Then we will say, *"My mouth will speak in praise of the Lord. Let every creature praise His holy name forever and ever"* (Ps. 145:21). Because God is the all-powerful Creator and Sustainer of everything, He alone is to be worshipped. Because God is just and merciful forgiving the repentant sinner, hearing the cry for mercy, He is to be worshiped.

The Rich Character of God

The many scriptural titles for Jesus bring out the richness of His character and underscore the nature of His mission: Lord, God, Word, Son of David, Son of Man, Firstborn from the dead, Image of God, Alpha and Omega, Savior, Redeemer, Light of the World, Lamb of God, High Priest, Good Shepherd, the Way, the Truth, and the Life, Author and Perfecter of our faith. These titles point to Jesus' role of mediator, one who stands between God and humanity to reveal the heart of God to His people and to make a way for sinful humans to come into His presence.

Jesus is the Word from God

John begins his gospel by saying that Jesus is *logos*, the Word. (John 1:1) But what did *"logos"* mean to a Jew? The Jew literate in the Hebrew Scriptures would associate Jesus with the creative power of God and the self-revelation of God in creation. James Montgomery Boice reminds us that the Jew would conclude that "Christ Himself was the focal point of God's revelation to man."[14] In the beginning God spoke words and His creation came into existence. God's words bring about concrete results as testified in Isaiah 55:10-11. God sent the Word i.e. Christ the *logos,* and the Word became flesh and made His dwelling among us (John 1:1; 14).

Heraclitus, the sixth-century B.C. philosopher of Greece, taught, "Life is not chaos because the change we see in life is no random change. It is ordered by divine reason or word, i.e. the logos—the creative and controlling mind of God." J.C.Ryle paraphrases John 1:1, "Listen, you Greeks, the very thing that has most occupied your philosophical thought and about which you have all been writing for centuries, the Logos of God, this word, this controlling power of the universe and man's mind has now come to earth as a man, and we have beheld him, full of grace and truth."[15]

Plato, we are told, once turned to that little group of philosophers and students that had gathered around him during the Golden Age in Athens and said, "It may be that some day there will come forth from God a Word, a Logos, who will reveal all mysteries and make everything plain." Now John is saying, "Yes, Plato, the Logos has come; now God is revealed to us perfectly." God, in Christ, has become man.[16]

Jesus is the Prophet -Teacher from God

Jesus the Christ is the Prophet of God who teaches us authoritatively about Himself, about His mission and about our place in God's world order (Matt. 7:21-29; John 6:35-40). He is LORD.[17] The word "Lord" stands for "master". However, Jesus' title is "LORD" which means, "I AM the way, the truth, and the life." (John 14:6). Jesus Himself said: "I tell you the truth: before Abraham was born, I AM!" (John 8:58) Jesus is God the Son, the One equal with the Father (John 10:30).

The prophetic ministry of Jesus Christ is authoritative. Jesus is not a mere man but the God-man who reveals God to us. In our day Jesus reveals God to us through His Holy Spirit who communicates the person of Christ to our minds and hearts through the Scriptures. "Preachers may set the food of the word before you, and carve it out for you, but it is only Christ who can cause you to taste it" (Thomas Watson). When Christ teaches us, we obey His authority. False prophets do not have authority. They may instruct and manipulate, but they have no authority over conscience and will. They may teach Christian virtues and are skillful in showing us how to behave, but only Christ effectively changes our wills. When Christ teaches, he not only informs us but He moves our wills, making us willing to learn. He transforms us by giving us the insight and the power to put His teaching into practice.

Even though we are by nature dead in spirit, unfit for being taught, Christ teaches the spiritually dead and brings them to life. Just as He told Lazarus to come out of the grave so that a dead and rotting Lazarus heard and came out, so Christ's teaching gives life to the dead soul. *"I am the resurrection and the life"* is thus another title Jesus gave Himself (John 11:25).

Christ the Prophet from God Teaches Us about Our Place in God's World

Jesus came into this world from God the Father to do His will. Jesus came to reverse the human condition after Adam's rebellion had brought God's curse on creation. He came to redeem sinners from emptiness and self-centeredness. Man was created in God's image, but rebelled against God and so was handed over to Satan, sin, and violence. Christ removed God's wrath on creation by crushing Satan's head by His death and resurrection. He put right the relationship between repentant sinners and God. Jesus gives us peace by renewing us and restoring us to God. Being with us inseparably forever, He equips us by His teaching and His indwelling power to bring renewal and restoration to the portion of the world in which we live. *"We are Christ's workmanship, created in Christ Jesus for good works, which God prepared beforehand so that we would walk in them"* (Eph. 2:10). Christ works to restore us to be like him.

The better one gets to know Christ, the more one becomes like Him (Phil. 3:10) since God created man in His image. When man sinned, the image of God in man was marred. Adam's children were born in the image of their fallen father, (Gen. 5:1, 3) but in spite of the ravages of sin, man still bears the image of God. (Gen. 9:6; Jas. 3:9) We were *formed* in God's image and *deformed* from God's image by sin; but, through Jesus Christ, we can be *transformed* into God's image!

Warren Wiersbe, explains the renewal work of Christ by referring to Colossians 3:10, saying, "The believer has once and for all put on the 'new man' (*neos*), and, as a consequence, he is being renewed (*kainos*). There is a change in quality for he is becoming like Jesus Christ. The 'new Man' is Jesus Christ, the last Adam, (1 Cor. 15:45) the Head of the new creation (2 Cor. 5:17).[18]

As we grow in knowledge of the Word of God, we will be transformed by the Spirit of God to share in the glorious image of God (2 Cor. 3:18). God transforms us by the renewing of our minds, (Rom. 12:2) and this involves the study of God's Word. It is the truth that sets us free from the old life (John 8:31-32).

It is wrong to build the worship of the church on anything other than Jesus Christ, His person and His work. Ministries that are built on human distinctions such as race, color, or social standing, are not biblical. One of the evidences of spiritual growth and the renewing of the mind is the willingness to receive and love all who sincerely know Christ and seek to glorify Him. When we genuinely seek Christ, fellowship with Him, and avoid all that displeases Christ, we discover the possibility of real worship and fellowship with one another. It is Christ in us, the hope of glory (Col. 1:27b), who calls us to love Him in obedience to His teaching.

How Do You Respond to Christ's Teaching?

The one who hears Christian teaching and never gets beyond hearing is like a foolish man who builds his house upon the sand (Matt. 7:26-27). He satisfies himself with listening and approving, but he goes no further. He flatters himself perhaps that all is right with his soul because he has feelings, convictions, and desires of a spiritual kind in which he rests. He never really breaks off from sin, casts aside the spirit of the world, lays hold of Christ, and takes up the cross. He is a hearer of truth but nothing more. The man who hears Christian teaching and practices what he hears is like a wise man that builds his house upon a rock (Matt. 7:24-25). He does not content himself with merely listening to exhortations to repent, believe in Christ, and live a holy life. He actually turns from sin, believes in Christ, ceases to do evil, and learns to do that which is considered good. He abhors that which is sinful and cleaves to that which is good. He is a doer as well as a hearer (Jas. 1:22).

Warning! The Lord Jesus Christ is Judge of all

Not everyone who says "Lord, Lord," will enter the kingdom of heaven (Matt. 7:22). Not all who profess and call themselves Christians will be saved. More is required than most people seem to think is necessary to save a soul. We may be baptized in the name of Christ and boast confidently of our church membership. We may possess head-knowledge and be quite satisfied with our own information. We may even be teachers of others and do many wonderful works in connection with our church. But the honest question is practical: "Am I doing the will of God the Father in heaven? Do I truly hate and forsake my sin, truly believe on Christ, and seek to live a holy and humble life?"

Remember, it is Christ, the Prophet of God through his Holy Spirit who communicates Christ's work to our minds and hearts by and with the Scriptures. The best safeguard against false belief is the regular study of the Word of God, with prayer for instruction from the Holy Spirit. The Bible is a lamp to our feet and a light to our path (Ps. 119:105). It is neglect of the Bible that makes so many prey to the false teachers. Study the Scriptures, not other writings that claim your attention. Beware of false prophets and guard your hearts against a false profession of being a follower of Christ.

Christ alone can give you understanding of Himself. Matthew 7:22-23 reads, *"Many will say to me on that day, `Lord, Lord, did we not prophesy in your name, and in your name drive out demons and perform many miracles?' Then I will tell them plainly, `I never knew you. Away from me, you evildoers!'"*

His authority will be seen at the final judgment. Calling Him Lord will not be reason to escape His judgment words, *"Depart from me, You who practice lawlessness*" (Matt. 7:23). What evidence will Christ accept on that *"day in which He will judge the world in righteousness?"* (Acts 17:31). Christ, God's Prophet, teaches us in Matthew 7:21 *"… he who does the will of My Father who is in heaven."*

How Do I Get to Know God's Will?

Christ's mission as Prophet of God is to make His will known to us. In John 6:38-40 Jesus tells us what the Father's will is. *"I have come down from heaven not to do my will but to do the will of him who sent me. And this is the will of him who sent me, that I shall lose none of all that he has given me, but raise them up at the last day. For my Father's will is that everyone who looks to the Son and believes in him shall have eternal life, and I will raise him up at the last day."*

Belief in Jesus is like a rope of three strands. First, know who He is and what He did to satisfy God's justice in the place of sinners. Second, assent to His authority and commit to Him. Third, trust in Him alone for everything pertaining to your life. Jesus is the "*logos*" of God, the controlling power of the universe and man's mind. Only when you yield to Him, serve Him, and confess your dependency on Him, will you find your significance and purpose in life.

Chapter Three

How should We Worship God?

We worship God with our focus on the Lord Jesus Christ. The word "Christ" is Greek for "messiah", literally "the anointed One."[19] Christ is the one called by God to reveal God, to mediate the grace of God, and to rule in order to bring *shalom* wholeness to the world. Because the Christian is united to Christ (Gal. 2:20; Col. 1:27b), the believer shares in Christ's anointing. The Christian is anointed to confess Christ's name, to present himself to Christ as a living sacrifice of thanks, to strive with a good conscience against sin and the devil in this life, and afterward to reign with Christ over all creation for all eternity. Paul reminds believers "to *offer (their) bodies as living sacrifices, holy and pleasing to God—this is your spiritual act of worship* (Rom. 12:1).

As Christians we bring our worship to Almighty God, the Great *I AM* through Jesus Christ. His work on the cross on our behalf reconciles the sole just and righteous One to sinners. Since sinners are set right by God it is possible for us to live in Christ's righteousness.

> *The God-who-sets-things-right, witnessed by Moses and the prophets whose witness we read about, has become Jesus who-sets-things-right for us and for everyone who believes in him. Since we have compiled a long and sorry record as sinners and have proven that we are utterly incapable of living the glorious lives that God wills for us, God, out of sheer generosity, put us in right standing with himself. God restored us to how we are to be before him by means of Jesus Christ when he sacrificed Jesus on behalf of the sinners who would believe in him. Through the punishment of Jesus as the payment of the world's sins, God set the world in the clear with himself*[20]
>
> *(Acts 3:21-25).*

Serving God in His world is Worship

There is a close link in the Scriptures between the ideas of worship and service. In the Old Testament the words of Joshua to the people are that they cannot serve the Lord because he is a holy God. Joshua instructs them to throw away their gods. The response of the people is *"We will serve the Lord our God and obey him"* (Jos. 24:19-24). The Hebrew word for serve is translated into the Greek as *latreian* (which can be translated as service or worship).

The King James Version translates *latreian* in Romans 12:1 *"...present your bodies as a living sacrifice wholly and acceptable unto God—which is your reasonable service."* The New International Version translates it *"...this is your spiritual act of worship."* Jesus instructs us that when we do an act of mercy to the *"least of one of these my brethren, you have done it unto me"* (Matt. 25:40). Serving the needy in mercy in the name of Christ is accepted as worship by Jesus. There is no dichotomy between service and worship. So when we are serving the King we are at the same time worshiping the King. *"Through Jesus, therefore, let us continually offer to God a sacrifice of praise—the fruit of our lips that confess his name. And do not forget to do good and to share with others, for with such sacrifices God is pleased"* (Heb. 13:15). The sacrifices of doing good and sharing with others are the priestly work of believers offered as worship to God.

Christ's Sacrifice unlocks the door to worship God

Jesus' death on the cross for sinners is Christ's priestly work. Because a priest is a man appointed to act for others in things pertaining to God, He is a mediator. A mediator is a connector. Christ connects humanity with God. Christ is both our priest and our mediator who fulfilled His work in two ways: (1) He offered Himself as the true sacrifice for sin, which the Old Testament priests could not do, and (2) He intercedes for His people in heaven. Hebrews 7:24-25 reads, *". . . because Jesus lives forever, he has a permanent priesthood. Therefore, he is able to save completely those who come to God through him, because he always lives to intercede for them."*

The worship rituals and practices of the Old Testament pointed to Christ. Under the Old Testament system, the priests of Israel were required to offer a sacrifice for sins. According to Leviticus 16:6, only the Old Testament high priest could go into the Holy of Holies on the Day of Atonement. There he would offer sacrifices for all sin committed by all the people during that year. But the sacrifices of the earthly priest were inadequate and incomplete. The blood of animals could not take away sins.

Micah 6:6-7, states: *"With what shall I come before the LORD and bow down before the exalted God? Shall I come before him with burnt offerings, with calves a year old? Will the Lord be pleased with thousands of rams, with ten thousand rivers of oil? Shall I offer my firstborn for my transgression, the fruit of my body for the sin of my soul?"*

The repeated offerings of the priests of the past made evident the very fact that these offerings were insufficient. Hebrews 10:3-7 states that *"those sacrifices are an annual reminder of sins, because it is impossible for the blood of bulls and goats to take away sins. Therefore, when Christ came into the world, he said: 'Sacrifice and offering you do not desire, but a body you prepared for me; with burnt offerings and sin offerings you were not pleased. Then I said, "Here I am, it is written about me in the scroll, I have come to do your will, O God."' Unlike the other high priests, Christ does not need to offer sacrifices day after day, first for His own sins, and then for the sins of the people'* (Heb. 7:27). His sacrifice is complete.

Christ's Sacrifice Satisfies God's Justice

The New Testament worship ritual focuses on Christ, the Lamb of God, as the substitutionary sacrifice for sinners. God's word tells us: *"Such a high priest meets our need - one who is holy, blameless, pure, set apart from sinners, exalted above the heavens"* (Heb. 7:26). *"…we have been made holy through the sacrifice of the body of Jesus Christ once for all"* (Heb. 10:10). *"The point of what we are saying is this. We have a high priest, who sat down at the right hand of the throne of the Majesty in heaven, and who serves…"* on our behalf (Heb. 8:1-2).

The evidence the sacrifice of Jesus is complete and eternal is that He has risen from the dead and ascended into heaven where He rules at the right hand of God. God the Righteous One accepted the sacrifice of Jesus as final and completely perfect to pardon all who trust in Christ. From heaven He has sent His Holy Spirit, the Christians' counselor, who convicts us of our guilt in regard to our sin and Christ's righteousness and His judgment on our sin (John 16:8). The Holy Spirit does not come with an independent message but He takes the words of Christ and makes them known to us (John 16:15). Christ is still our focus in all of life as the mediator between humanity and God the Father.

The Old Testament sacrifices were a shadow of things to come. Jesus Himself is the perfect priest and the perfect sacrifice. Christ's death was the atonement by which God declares the sinner righteous. The author of Hebrews explained. *"But when Christ came as high priest of the good things that are already here…he entered once for all into the Holy Place, once for all by his own blood, having obtained eternal redemption"* (Heb. 9:11-12).

Because of God's Mercy We Confess Our Sin in Worship

God's work in us explains why worship requires confession of sin and constant dependence on Christ. Confessing our sin is the response of a grateful heart to God's love for us through the atoning work of Christ Jesus.

We need to understand the destructive power of sin in order to appreciate God's mercy. Sin leads us to rebel against God—to be self-sufficient and independent of God, but God's love in Christ deals with our rebellious nature. Sin brings death, God's judgment! *"The soul that sins shall die"* (Ezek. 18:4). What is the sinner's escape from God's judgment on man who sins constantly? Escape comes by taking refuge in Jesus who deals with sin by His death and resurrection. God is so very loving, gracious, and compassionate that He sent His Son to offer Himself as an innocent substitute in the sinner's place. Jesus was, and is, for all who call on Him and trust on Him, Savior! A true Christian worships God with deepest gratitude in dependence on Christ who sacrificed Himself once for all for all His people. Confessing our sin is a way of thanking God for His mercy to us in Christ upon whom we rest and through whom we sin less and less.

Christ's Continual Intercession makes our Worship Acceptable to God

> He is able to save completely, those who come to God through him, because he always lives to intercede for them.
>
> *(Heb. 7:25)*

Completely means fully and completely for all time. Jesus continually lives with the purpose of interceding for those who come to God through Him. He knows His sheep by name. He came to find His straying sheep, to seek the lost and bring them into His fold. He loves them with an eternal love and will not forsake them. Nothing can snatch them out of His hand. This is the result of His intercession for His own before his Father's throne.

His act of intercession is to intervene between God and sinners with a view to reconcile differences. Intercession was often a petition brought before a king or someone in authority on the behalf of another. The use of intercession is also a way to pray to God for others as Paul urged, *"that requests, prayers, intercession and thanksgiving be made for everyone…"* (1 Tim. 2:1). Paul makes it perfectly plain that Christ is the only mediator and intercessor. To rely upon angels or saints or any other being for intercession is not only futile, but it also betrays a failure of confidence in the adequacy of Christ as our intercessor.

Jesus prayed for His church the very night He submitted Himself to His Father's will to be crucified at the hands of Romans and Jews. John 17 gives us an idea of Jesus' intercession for the Christian. His prayer is that they might be made the kind of men and women He would have them be, that is, men and women in whom the characteristics of His church are evident: joy, holiness, truth, mission, unity, and love.[21] The apostle John speaks of Jesus as our advocate in 1 John 2:1-2: *"But, if anybody does sin, we have one who speaks to the Father in our defense—Jesus Christ, the Righteous One. He is the atoning sacrifice for our sins…"* The Lord Jesus pleads the sacrifice of Himself as the foundation of our coming to God in confidence, thus finding God's mercy to meet our need.

How does all this affect the church?

The church is a congregation of God's people who come to pray earnestly for other members. They treat one another so graciously that they intermingle more like grapes on a vine than marbles in a child's pocket. According to Ann Ortlund's analogy of the "grapes and the marbles"[22], they would not abrasively bump into each other; they would fit together as grapes on a vine. God's people would be authentic worshipers who love the Father, Son, and Holy Spirit with all their hearts and their neighbors as themselves.[23]

Honoring Christ Our King

Christ is not only our mediator; He is also our Priest, Prophet and King. We have become much more familiar with the fact that Christ is our High Priest and also our Prophet; however, the kingship of Christ is seldom reflected upon by the church. We confess it when we sing the hymn *"Crown Him with Many Crowns the Lamb upon His Throne…"* We gladly confess that we crown Him Prophet, Priest, and King. Yet the meaning of Christ's kingship can still be somewhat remote in our thinking. The Westminster Confession of Faith coming out of the English reformation makes this truth quite explicit.[24]

God was pleased, in His eternal purpose, to choose and ordain the Lord Jesus, His only begotten Son, to be the mediator between God and man. As the mediator, He is the prophet, priest, and king, the head and Savior of the church, the heir of all things, and the judge of the world. God gave to him from all eternity a people to be his seed and to be by him, in time, redeemed, called, justified, sanctified and glorified.

We teach our children a simpler statement of this truth in the Westminster Shorter Catechism: "How does Christ execute the office of a king? Answer: Christ executes the office of a king, in subduing us to himself, in ruling and defending us, and in restraining and conquering all his and our enemies."[25]

The Biblical Story of Christ's Kingship

God spoke through the prophet Nathan (around 900 B.C.) to great King David, saying *"Your house and your kingdom shall endure before me forever; your throne shall be established forever"* (2 Sam. 7:16). As time unfolded it appeared that the ruling house of David was in decline under King Ahaz. God, then, sent the prophet Isaiah (around 700 B.C.) to give more detail of His promise to David, saying, *"For a child will be born to us…the government will rest on his shoulders; and his name will be called Wonderful Counselor, Mighty God, Eternal Father, Prince of Peace. There will be no end to the increase of his government or of peace on the throne of David, and over his kingdom…The zeal of the Lord of hosts will accomplish this"* (Isa. 9:6-7).

A later prophet sent by God was Micah who prophesied around 680 B.C. He taught of the birthplace of the "The Man Born to be King" (Dorothy Sayers' title of her play of Jesus' Passion and Suffering),[26] saying,

> *But as for you, Bethlehem Ephrathah, too little to be among the clans of Judah, from you one will go forth for me to be ruler in Israel. His goings forth are from long ago, from the days of eternity.*
>
> (Mic. 5:2)

Years passed before God spoke of the King who rules over mankind through the prophet Daniel (around 530 B.C.) in these words, *"I kept looking in the night visions, and behold, with the clouds of heavens one like a Son of Man was coming, and he came up to the Ancient of Days and was presented before him. And to him was given dominion, glory and a kingdom that all the peoples, nations and men of every language might serve him. His dominion is an everlasting dominion which will not pass away; and his kingdom is one which will not be destroyed"* (Dan. 7:13-14).

It was John the Baptist (around A.D. 30) who identified Jesus as the Judge and Ruler of all the earth, promised by God through the prophets. John witnessed God Himself declaring that Jesus was His very own Son. Mark records, *"In those days Jesus came from Nazareth in Galilee and was baptized by John in the Jordan. Immediately coming up out of the water, he saw the heavens opening, and the Spirit like a dove descending upon him; and a voice came out of the heavens: 'You are my beloved Son, in you I am well pleased'"* (Mark 1:9-11). *"After a time spent in the wilderness being tempted by the Devil, Jesus began to preach and say, 'Repent for the kingdom of heaven is at hand'"* (Matt. 4:17; Mark 1:15).

The apostle John, in a God-given vision, saw Christ Jesus at the end of the ages seated on a white horse coming in kingly splendor.

His name is called the Word of God. And the armies that are in heaven, clothed in linen, white and clean, were following him on white horses. From his mouth comes a sharp sword, so that with it he may strike down the nations, and he will rule them with a rod of iron; and he treads the wine press of the fierce wrath of God, the Almighty. And on his robe and on his thigh he has a name written, 'King of kings, and Lord of lords.'

(Rev. 19:11-16)

Jesus is the King of kings

One of the clearest teachings and most quoted passages of the Old Testament by the New Testament authors on Christ's kingly rule is in Psalm 110 (Matt. 22:44; Mark 12:36; Luke 20:42-43; Acts 2:34-35; 7:56; 1 Cor. 15:25; Eph. 1:20; Col. 3:1; Heb. 1:3, 13; 12:2; 1 Pet. 3:22; also Hebrews 5:6; 7:17, 21, 8:1; 10:11-13). James Montgomery Boice says, "Psalm 110 is entirely about a divine king who has been installed at the right hand of God in heaven and who is presently engaged in extending his spiritual rule throughout the whole earth. It tells us that this divine Messiah is also a priest, performing priestly functions, and that additionally he is a judge who at the end of time will execute a final judgment on the nations and rulers of this earth."[27]

Walter Chantry sees Psalm 110 as being exclusively about Christ. He divides it into four parts: namely, the powerful reign of Christ (v. 1), the spiritual reign of Christ (vv. 2-3), the priestly reign of Christ (v. 4), and the judicial reign of Christ (vv. 5-7)[28]. The reality of Jesus' kingship is not only the foundation of why we worship God through Christ, but it also is the basis by which his people are continually encouraged.

How Does King Jesus Rule His Creation?

Jesus, the believer's mediatorial King, rules creation through his people. According to Psalm 110 Jesus ascends to the throne of God (1, 2(a)); He assigns His people as stewards over His creation (3); and He assures his people of victory by his presence (5, 6).

Psalm 110

1. *The LORD said to my Lord:*
"Sit here at my right hand,
Until I make your foes a stool
on which your feet may stand."
2. *The LORD will make your reign*
extend from Zion's hill;
With royal power you'll rule among
those who oppose your will.
3. *When you display your power,*
Your people flock to you;
At dawn, arrayed in holiness,
Your youth will come like dew.
4. *Unchangeable the LORD*
With solemn purpose swore:
"Just like Melchizedek you are
a priest for evermore.
5. *The Lord's at your right hand;*
There he will ever stay.
He on his day of wrath will crush
The kings who bar his way.
6. *The nations he will judge;*
The dead in heaps will lie.
The mighty of the earth he'll crush –
all who his rule defy.

7.   A brook beside the way
his thirst will satisfy;
And, thus refreshed, he will with joy
Lift up his head on high.

(The Free Church of Scotland
Paraphrases 2005)

Jesus the God-Man has ascended to God's throne. In Psalm 110:1 David says, *"The LORD (i.e. Yahweh, I AM) says to my (i.e. David's) Lord (i.e. Adonai— master), "sit at my (Yahweh's) right hand"*[29]. The right hand is the place of honor, power, and privilege. The command to sit there gives the right and authority to occupy that position and the ruling function that accompanies it. The command to sit is not only a royal privilege and position that is referred to; it is a divine position! It is *Yahweh* who speaks; it is *Yahweh's* right hand; it is the reign of *Yahweh* that is transferred to '*my Lord*.'

The throne of David represents *Yahweh's* throne. Jesus descended from David and was thus an heir to David's throne. David believed *Yahweh's* promise and hoped for its fulfillment. Jesus was the fulfillment. He is the one who will rule on David's throne forever. The apostle Peter on the Day of Pentecost explained the meaning of this verse in Acts 2:29-31, 34-36, *"Brothers, I may confidently say to you regarding the patriarch David, that he both died and was buried, and his tomb is with us to this day. And so, because he was a prophet and knows that God had sworn to him with an oath to seat one of his descendants on his throne, he looked ahead and spoke of the resurrection of the Christ…This Jesus God raised up again to which we are all witnesses…It was not David who ascended into heaven, but he himself says, 'The Lord said to my lord, sit at my right hand until I make your enemies a footstool for your feet.' Therefore…know for certain that God has made Him both Lord and Christ—this Jesus whom you crucified."*

Jesus Lives and Rules through His People

Jesus shares in rule over creation with His Father from the throne of God; the Holy Spirit is sent to empower the witnesses of God's saving grace, those for whom Jesus died to save from Satan, sin, and death. Jesus first exercises His rule by drawing the individual to faith in Himself; He then empowers that person with His indwelling presence (John 14:16-20) to commence His Lordship over all of life. Jesus' throne holds sway over the believer for this present life and the life of eternal reward.

A king is to be honored, confessed, obeyed and worshiped.[30] *"If you confess with your mouth 'Jesus is Lord,' and believe in your heart that God raised him from the dead, you will be saved"* (Rom. 10:8). If you belong to the risen Christ then you serve King Jesus in His world.

Jesus assigns His people to be stewards over His creation. Psalm 110:2 teaches that Christ's rule comes from Zion which is described in Hebrews 12:22-23 as *"the city of the living God, the heavenly Jerusalem, and to myriads of angels, to the general assembly and church of the firstborn who are enrolled in heaven…"* Christians, those in whom Christ dwells (Col. 1:27; Gal. 2:20), "rule in the midst of His enemies." God has made believers in Christ to be kings with Christ. Revelation 5:10 teaches that Jesus was *"slain and purchased with his blood, for God, men from every tribe and tongue and people and nation, making them to be a kingdom and priests to our God; and these will reign/rule upon the earth."*

Walter Chantry says rightly that the world is "in desperate need of a spiritual church using spiritual weapons to fight a spiritual war, under the spiritual reign of Christ."[31] Informed by God's Word, Christians must endeavor to persuade others of the truth, pray, bring every thought captive to Christ and work for the restoration of creation.

Psalm 110:3 reads: *"Your people will volunteer freely in the day of your power. In holy array from the womb of the dawn, your youth are to you as the dew."* As refreshing dew comes at dawn, so the youth of the covenant people of God will come to the sovereign Master, follow Him, and serve Him. Thus, under the sovereign Lord's exercise of His scepter, both the older and younger members of the covenant community will participate in His "kingship" and share in the assured victory over His enemies at the renewal of all things (Matt. 19:28).

Jesus assures his people of victory over evil. Psalm 110:5-7 tells us that the King-Priest is at the right hand of *Yahweh* and that indicates the complete victory of the Sovereign Master and the annihilation of His enemies. The kings of all the nations in the earth will have their heads shattered. With *Yahweh's* mandate, power, and assurance of victory, Christ will go forward and achieve victory. The reference in verse 7 is to the ability to refresh oneself during pursuit to complete victory. Refreshed, strengthened, with head held high, victory is achieved. The King-Priest will respond by performing His duties and thus serve the cause of *Yahweh* and His covenant people. His Kingdom will come!

Today Jesus is at God's right hand, ruling over all things in heaven and on earth by His Spirit. Jesus *is* Lord, and God has made Him such. We can fight that Lordship or be broken by it – Christ's enemies will be made His footstool. Or we can submit to His Lordship in humble obedience with praise.

Anyone who has caught a glimpse of the sovereign might and heavenly splendor of Christ will want to imitate the saints of ages past. It is only appropriate to worship Christ with deep reverence. We can pour out our love in recognition of His personal relationship with us and worship the King all glorious above and marvelously sing of His power and love. This we do because He is our Lord and King.

"…Begin to think of Jesus, as he is today, exalted to a position of honor at God's right hand. Most people's image of Jesus is that of a baby in a manger. It is a sentimental picture best reserved for Christmas and other sentimental times. Others picture him hanging on a cross. That too is sentimental, though it is sentimentality of a different pious sort. Jesus is not in a manger today. That is past. No more is he hanging on a cross. That too is past since Jesus came once to die for sin and afterwards He ascended to heaven to share in the fullness of God's power and great glory. When Stephen, the first martyr, had his dying vision of the exalted Christ it was of Jesus *"standing at the right hand of God to receive him into heaven"* (Acts 7:55). When John, on the Isle of Patmos, had his vision of Jesus it was of one who is God. The apostle was so overcome by Jesus' heavenly splendor that he *"fell at his feet as though dead"* (Rev. 1:17).

If we did really understand who Jesus is and where He is now we would worship Him with greater reverence[32] in His service.

Christians are the Lord's Bondservants

The Apostle Paul describes himself a bondservant of the Lord (Rom. 1:1). A bondservant of Jesus is one who is able to go free but chooses to remain in bondage to His Lord. A bondservant freely and gladly submits to the Lord Jesus Christ to worship and serve Him without reservation. Paul also says that he is an example of the believer in this matter. He in turn gives the same advice to Timothy. *"Don't let anyone look down upon you because you are young, but set an example for the believer in speech, in life, in love, in faith and in purity"* (1 Tim. 4:12). It is the responsibility of all who own Jesus as Lord to follow in this pattern of life. Being a bondservant begins with submission in worship to the Lord. The result is the transformation of a life of service. George Matheson understood this clearly when he wrote,[33]

> *Make me a captive, Lord,*
> *And then I shall be free.*
> *Force me to render up my sword,*
> *And I shall conqueror be.*
> *I sink in life's alarms*
> *When by myself I stand;*
> *Imprison me within thine arms,*
> *And strong shall be my hand.*
>
> *My will is not my own*
> *Till thou has made it thine;*
> *If it would reach a monarch's throne,*
> *It must its crown resign.*
> *It only stands unbent*
> *Amid the clashing strife,*
> *When in thy bosom it has leant,*
> *And found in thee its life.*

Chapter Four

Giving Yourself to God in Worship

Worship is an attitude of the heart that demands exercising of the mind, spirit, and body. A common perception of worship is that we worship in order to get. We look for some blessing, ecstatic feeling, or insight into Scripture. If our expectations are not realized in the sermons or the music, we leave feeling empty or, even worse, betrayed. In reality we go to worship not to get but to give. We are engaging in worship in order to give God the glory that is due to Him. Because we are in a love relationship with God through Jesus we come to show Him our love along with others who love Him. The goal is to give to Him in worship and the byproduct is the receiving of God's blessing. It's all about our relationship with God. It is important not to confuse the goal with the consequences or to lose the reality of the relationship with our Lord and Savior.

Love relationships take effort

We have the expectation that God will speak to our hearts through the Scripture, sermon and spiritual songs. God speaks to our hearts by His Spirit in and through the written words of Scripture. Our minds engage the Scripture that instructs us to acknowledge God's presence with us in worship. God's revealed word through the prophets and apostles of Jesus about Himself teaches us that God is totally self-sufficient, eternal, infinite and unchanging in his Being; therefore, His wisdom, holiness, power, justice, goodness and truth remain constant. This should encourage us to want to develop our relationship with Him even though He is far greater than we can imagine or ever know. Yet we should not limit His majesty to the imaginations of our small minds. This limitation is nothing but idolatry. We must resist the temptation to make Him in our image and have Him do what we demand. Sir Alfred Tennyson in his poem, *In Memoriam*[34], captures this concept for us.

> *Our little systems have their day;*
> *They have their day and cease to be:*
> *They are but broken lights of thee,*
> *And thou O Lord, art more than they.*

Worship is our work of responding to God's grace to us in Christ Jesus with thankful hearts. We know that we can only come to God through the atoning work of Jesus, whose death on the cross satisfies Divine justice. We know that Jesus rose from the dead and ascended into heaven where he always lives to pray for all who come to God through him. As Hebrews 12:22-24 states:

> *But you have come to Mount Zion, to the heavenly Jerusalem, the city of the living God. You have come to thousands upon thousands of angels in joyful assembly, to the church of the firstborn, whose names are written in heaven. You have come to God, the judge of all men, to the spirits of righteous men made perfect, to Jesus the mediator of a new covenant.*

We are to worship God acceptably with reverence and awe, for our *"God is a consuming fire."* We worship Christ for standing in the presence of God for us so that God's holiness will not consume us.

Paul gives guidance on how to worship God acceptably with reverence and awe in his instructions to the congregation of believers in Philippi (4:4 ff), *"Rejoice in the Lord always. I will say it again: Rejoice! Let your gentleness be evident to all. The Lord is near. Do not be anxious about anything, but in everything, by prayer and petition, with thanksgiving, present your requests to God. And the peace of God, which transcends all understanding, will guard your hearts and your minds in Christ Jesus."*

Paul is telling us to rejoice no matter what we feel. How is that possible? His words, *Rejoice in the Lord* provide the answer. This joy is not based on how we feel about our personal circumstances, but on the fact of our fellowship with Christ, and on the truth about Him. Paul is saying, that we will be able to taste joy whatever the circumstances.

The joy of prayer in the worship of God
Worship is the response of the heart to God's goodness in prayer. In prayer we offer up our "desires to God, for things that are agreeable to His will, in the name of Christ with confession of our sins, and thankful acknowledgement of His mercies."[35] In Jesus we rejoice. In Jesus we respond to God's mercies and therefore approach God joyfully.

Prayer is not merely a listing of needs but an opening of the heart to God that includes praising Him for all He is and all He has done for us. We show our adoration of God in our prayers of praise. The very essence of worship is praise or telling God how wonderful He is. In everything, we acknowledge Him as Lord. We are His through our union with Christ, who, by His Spirit, lives in us. We present our requests to God in Jesus' Name.

When we pray in Jesus' name, we pray for that which is pleasing to Him not primarily for what will make us happy. In prayer, as in all worship, we seek what pleases the Lord, not what pleases ourselves. We know that Jesus loves us and desires our happiness. This fact is as relevant for prayer as it is for worship in general. One day He will make us ecstatic with unending joy but the road to that happiness is often paved with suffering. Our prayers accept His will in that regard as in all others. With Jesus himself, we pray, "*Yet not as I will, but as you will*" (Matt. 26:39). We should, therefore, always seek to shape our prayers in line with the word of God and pray for the blessings that God has promised us.

What about the things that God has not specifically promised in Scripture? Is it right to pray for a job, healing of a particular illness, or an opportunity to share the gospel with a neighbor? Certainly it is, as long as our prayer does not arise from a sinful desire. Jesus prayed that somehow it might not be necessary for Him to suffer on the cross (Matt. 26:39). That was a Godly desire. It is right for us to seek relief from pain and suffering; in that sense, such a prayer is in God's will. But God, in His higher purposes, does not always grant relief from suffering (2 Cor. 12:7-10).

There are wonderful promises in Scripture to those who pray in Jesus' name, but often God says, "no". Does God not contradict Jesus' promise in John 14:14, *"You may ask me for anything in my name, and I will do it."* Keep two principles in mind: First, God's "no" is only temporary. Every true prayer will be answered in the glory of the new heaven and the new earth. In that kingdom, every disease will be healed, all of God's elect will be saved, and God's people will live as kings. If the ultimate prayer of our hearts is that God's will be done, and if we are willing to hold loosely to our specific concerns for the overall good of the kingdom (Matt. 6:33), then even in this world our prayers will always be answered.

Joy in worship in the use of our wills and emotions

Sometimes we have been misled into thinking of joy as a matter of feeling and spontaneous emotion. This is a distortion of biblical teaching. It is true that God made men and women capable of thinking, willing, and feeling; but in the divine design, our thinking is always to be informed, shaped, and governed by His revealed truth in Scripture.

We were created to think God's thoughts after Him. Such thought processes inevitably inform, influence, and direct our power to exercise our wills. We understand what is right and good. Therefore, we commit our wills to accomplishing it. In turn, our feelings are molded by what we think and will. Our feelings and emotions are not isolated from our thoughts and will, but rather guided by them.

In a rightly ordered life, emotions or feelings are directed to what is good and gracious; these things are desired and loved. Because of the rebellion of sin we know that the rightly ordered life was overturned and that has affected our reasoning and minds. Our wills now tend to be dominated by our feelings, our thoughts ruled by our wills. Because of sin we are able to rejoice only when we feel good; but, by contrast it is our fellowship with Jesus Christ that enables us to rejoice no matter how we feel.

Worship then is not limited to our feelings. Worship demands that we use our minds to direct our feelings. This direction requires work. We are to work at worship and use our wills to approach God. Will directed to action is expressed in feeling.

Finding peace and joy in prayers of confession

We know that as sinners we are saved by grace; yet when we approach God, we want to recall our sins because they have offended Him. We approach God only on the basis of the blood of Jesus shed for us. So therefore, we approach God in the name of Jesus (meaning we trust in Him and know we are inseparably united to Him). If we love Jesus, we will regularly admit our sins, grieve over them and be sorry that we have displeased Him; then we will ask God's forgiveness for the sake of Jesus.

Sincere confession involves repentance that is more than feeling sorry for sin, more than asking for forgiveness; it is an actual turning from sin that is behavioral, not just mental. If we come to God claiming that we hate our sin and desire to be rid of it through Jesus, then at the same time we must have the serious purpose of forsaking that sin. Otherwise our confession is only words. Remember that worship is the work of your mind, body, and heart. It is action. Confession without the action of bringing your behavior into line with God's teachings is not true worship.[36]

When Christ's teachings control our minds they will influence us more powerfully than our circumstances. People who are joyful are those who have been delivered from an obsession with themselves and their immediate circumstances. The joyful person extends gentleness to all because the joyful person knows that the Lord is near, or as Paul puts it, *"…Christ in you, the hope of glory"* (Col. 1:27), and knows that *"it is no longer I who live but Christ lives in me"* (Gal. 2:20).

When the Christian grieves over sin, Christ is near. As Psalm 34:18 says, *"The Lord is close to the brokenhearted and saves those who are crushed in spirit."*

Worship is opening the mind to God's grace, thinking God's thoughts after Him and rejoicing no matter what one's feelings. The result is that the joyful person is not likely to be dominated by anxiety.

How can one be free from anxiety?
The prescription is prayer. Paul states: *"Do not be anxious about anything, but in everything, by prayer and petition, with thanksgiving, present your requests to God. And the peace of God which transcends all understanding will guard your hearts and your minds in Christ Jesus"* (Phil. 4:6-7). We patiently spread our needs before God explaining our situation and expressing our anxieties.

Worship is the response of opening our hearts to God's grace in Christ by exercising our will and emotions in communicating with God in prayer.

Finding Joy in Worship by giving thanks to God

Remember that we owe everything we have and are to God. God owes us nothing. His blessings come to us because of His kindness. As sinners we deserve only death and endless punishment, yet God's blessings come to us by grace, His unmerited favor.

This is why our entire life is one of thanksgiving, a grateful response to God's kindness and infinite wise love. The bible's accounts of prayer abound with prayers of thanks to God for all His blessings. God's people rejoice even in suffering, as did the apostles after they had been flogged, *"because they had been counted worthy of suffering disgrace for the Name"* (Acts 5:41; Phil. 3:10; Col. 1:24; 1 Peter 1:6-9; 4:13). So we can thank God for allowing suffering into our lives according to His good purposes that will, in His time, not only lead to the end of all our sin and suffering but also draw us into a closer and deeper relationship with Him in the present.

Opening the heart to God's grace in Christ Jesus with thanksgiving is worship. Worshipers experience the mysterious peace of God, which transcends all understanding and guards their hearts and minds in Christ. A mind well layered with grace will worship joyfully in prayer and learn to say from the heart, with Job of old, *"Naked I came from my mother's womb, and naked I will depart. The Lord gave and the Lord has taken away; may the name of the Lord be praised"* (Job 1:21). Job said this after falling to the ground in worship. Our fellowship is with the Father and with his Son who speaks to the Father in our defense, Jesus Christ, the Righteous One, our Savior and the friend of sinners. Every moment of the Christian life is lived in fellowship with Christ. Every conflict, every pain, every disappointment and strain is met with the realization that we have a friend who sticks closer than a brother, namely Jesus Christ. Surely then He is worthy of all worship.

Warning! Rigid forms of worship often destroy joy in worship

Jesus confronted a religious group called the Pharisees (Matt. 15:3-6). He asked them a question relevant to the practice of some modern-day worship. He asks, *"Why do you break the command of God for the sake of your tradition?"* Then Jesus tells them that they have used their tradition of the interpretations of men to add statements to God's Scriptures in order to make sure that they will keep God's law and also allow themselves some freedom to do what Scriptures forbid. He says, *"For God said, 'Honor your father and mother' and 'anyone who curses his father or mother must be put to death.' But you say that if a man says to his father or mother, 'Whatever help you might otherwise have received from me is a gift devoted to God,' he is not to 'honor his father' with it. Thus you nullify the word of God for the sake of your tradition."*

The Pharisees held to the tradition of elders at the expense of God's written words. So Jesus asks, *"Why do you transgress the commandment of God for the sake of your tradition?"* He then points out their hypocritical practice. They take Exodus 20:12, the fifth commandment, and interpret it with 21:17 to say "whatever you would have gained from me is given to God so I need not honor you my parents."

There is a similar process that has unfolded over the years among some Christian groups that works against true joyful worship. The Pharisees took God's commandments and twisted them to satisfy their human ideas of religious practice in order to easily obey God's law. The result was that the Pharisees' religious practices became ritualistic. The ritual then became a tradition that resulted in binding the conscience of worshipers.

Soon the word of God is forgotten while the tradition becomes the law and rule of worship. The doctrines of men become the commandments to obey, while God's commandments are conveniently ignored. The end result is that the people practice a form of worship that is not directed by God; it is man-made worship that binds people's consciences and is just the opposite of *"worshiping God in Spirit and truth."*

The Pharisaical teachings were nothing more than behaviorism, a set of laws to practice that led to a form of outward behavior with a religious appearance. It proved to be a lip service, instead of a heart service.

We need to learn from this how easy we can make worship a ritualistic and rigid man-made form and lose the reality that acceptable worship is a matter of the heart from one *"who is humble and contrite in spirit and trembles at His word"* (Isa. 66:1-2).

Heart worship, the apostle Paul explains (Rom. 12:1), is a response *"...to God's mercy,"* and we are *"to offer (our) bodies as living sacrifices, holy and pleasing to God—this is your spiritual act of worship."* A simple outline of Romans helps us understand Paul's concept of worship. In chapters 1-11 we learn all God has done. In chapters 12-16 we respond in giving all that we are.

Worship of this sort is not something you switch on and off at a church service. It is all-of-life worship. In response to God's magnificent mercies, we gladly present all we have and all we are to God in our times of daily prayer, in our homes, our workplaces, and corporately in our local church's special Lord's Day gatherings.

Approaching the worship gathering with an expectant, grateful heart is living out the truth of Psalm 100:4 – *"Enter his gates with thanksgiving and his courts with praise; give thanks to him and praise his name."* We will be much less likely to criticize the way a service is conducted if we come with a thankful heart and will. A heart of gratitude shapes one's attitude of love for God and others.

When coming to worship with others ask yourself, "What kind of worship does God delight in?" and "How can I best serve and bless the people around me?" Keep away from the self-centered attitude that asks, "What will meet my need?"

How are we to prevent a deadening "tradition

of religious practice" from taking the place of God's revealed will in regard to worship? Isaiah (66:2) gives us a clue. He says the Lord who made all things *"looks to him who is humble and contrite of spirit and who trembles at His word".* Eugene Peterson renders this passage as, *"a person simple and plain, reverently responsive to what I say."*[37]

We need to understand what God's word has to say about His desires for us on how to approach Him in worship in the local gathering.

The Scripture and the Church Worship Gathering

John Frame's *Worship in Spirit and Truth*[38] is helpful here. "All of life is worship, in that we always seek to serve our Lord and to pay Him homage." *"All the world is his palace"* (Isa. 66:1). But when He meets with us, something special happens. The Bible uses the term "worship" to express that special situation.

From the beginning of the New Testament church, believers delighted in meeting together, and in those meetings they experienced unique blessings of the Spirit of God (Acts 1:6, 14; 2:42-47; 4:23-31; 5:42; 13:2; 20:7-12; 1 Cor. 11:18-34; 14:1-40). They met for prayer, teaching, and sacrament. They pronounced publicly in the meeting the judgments of church discipline (1 Cor. 5:4-5). The church received gifts for Christians in special need (1 Cor. 16:1-2). They exchanged the "holy kiss" (Rom. 16:16; 1 Cor. 16:20).

The New Testament does use Old Testament temple worship terminology for some things that we do at the corporate worship meeting. Our gifts can be *"a fragrant offering, an acceptable sacrifice, pleasing to God"* (Phil. 4:18; Heb. 13:16). Our praises are sacrifices (Heb. 13:15). Prayers in Scripture are often closely related to the smoke that arose from the altar of incense in the tabernacle and the temple (Ps. 141:2; Luke 1:10; Rev. 5:8; 8:3-4). Prayer is a lifting up of "holy hands" (1 Tim. 2:8). The word that we read and preach is "holy" (2 Tim. 3:16; 2 Pet. 2:21; 3:2). In Hebrews 4:12 that word pierces into our inmost parts: the language is that of sacrifice. The kiss by which New Testament Christians expressed their fellowship and unity was also "holy" (Rom. 16:16; 1 Cor. 16:20; 2 Cor. 13:12; 1 Thess. 5:26). We, as the church, are a holy temple (1 Cor. 3:17; Eph. 2:21; 5-27; Rev. 21:2, 10) and a holy priesthood (1 Pet. 2:5). In worship, we draw near to the heavenly Jerusalem, to God and the angels in joyful assembly (Heb. 12:22-24).

All of this points us in the direction of the true worship of God that flows from the joyful heart that is turned toward God. When our attitude in worship is pleasing to God we approach him with great confidence. We are called to offer to God spiritual sacrifices that are acceptable to God through Christ (1 Pet. 2:4). We have the assurance of God Himself that He receives these acts of worship. *"The sacrifices of God are a broken spirit; a broken and contrite heart, O God, you will not despise."*

Chapter Five

What To Do When
We Worship Together?

There is a definite place for Christians to meet together to experience God's presence and to worship Him. We call this the "worship service." God is present in a special way in the Christian meeting. When Christians worship as God commands them to worship, an unbeliever coming to the service will be given a strong example to worship, recognizing that *"God is really among you!"* (1 Cor.14:25). Therefore, the meeting is not something discretionary.

Many professing Christians today believe that they can go to church or not go as they please. They will go if they are not tired, or busy with something else, or working, or socializing, or watching a football game. For them the meeting itself has a very low priority. Usually this behavior is a result of not thinking through the issues dealt with in this booklet so far. This kind of behavior is unworthy of one who claims to be a follower of Jesus Christ the King of kings and Lord of lords. Some people try to make excuses for their behavior reasoning that true worship is in all of life, not in weekly meetings. They argue that they can worship God perfectly well in their own living rooms or on the golf course or even in bed. But God's word, through the writer of Hebrews, has a very different view. To Him the meeting is vitally important *"Let us not give up meeting together, as some are in the habit of doing, but let us encourage one another—and all the more as you see the Day approaching"* (Heb. 10:25).

God's Word gives us regulations for Worship

The Sovereign Creator, Lord God, demands that our worship be governed by His teachings. Isaiah tells us that God looks with favor on those who are humble and contrite in spirit – those who tremble at His word. If we neglect to worship God 'with reverence and awe' according to His teachings in Scripture, we provoke His anger and discipline rather than His blessing.

As we have already seen God condemns worship based on human ideas. Jesus affirmed God's words through the prophet Isaiah (29:13), *"These people come near to me with their mouth, honor me with their lips, but their hearts are far from me. Their worship of me is made up only of rules taught by men."* God's word regulates our worship both when we congregate and in all of life.

The delegates to the Westminster Assembly in 1648 wrote in the Confession of Faith "The acceptable way of worshiping the true God is instituted by Himself, and so limited by his own revealed will, that he may not be worshiped according to the imaginations and devices of men, or the suggestions of Satan, under any visible representative, or any other way not prescribed in the Holy Scripture."[39] This is often referred to as the "regulative principle" governing worship.

We recognize that human wisdom is needed to apply God's revealed word in the planning of worship. Scripture gives us the basic concepts, not the detailed direction in practice. The Westminster Confession of Faith says, "The whole counsel of God concerning all things necessary for his own glory, man's salvation, faith and life, is either expressly set down in Scripture, *or by good and necessary consequence may be deduced from Scripture*; unto which nothing at any time is to be added, whether by new revelation of the Spirit or traditions of men (John 6:45; 1 Cor. 1:9-12). Nevertheless, we acknowledge the inward illumination of the Spirit of God to be necessary for a saving understanding of such things as are revealed in the Word; and that *there are some circumstances concerning the worship of God and the government of the Church common to human actions and societies, which are to be ordered by the light of nature, and Christian prudence, according to the general rules of the Word, which are always observed* (1 Cor. 11:13-14, 14:26, 40).[40]

John Frame[41] reminds us that, "Scripture tells us to meet, but not when and where, so we must use our own judgment. Similarly, Scripture tells us to pray, but does not dictate to us all the specific words we should use, so we need to decide. Scripture tells us to honor our parents. It doesn't tell us how often to call our mothers or what to buy for their birthdays. We must make those decisions by godly application of Scripture to our situations." The "regulative principle" for worship is no different from the principles that God calls us to apply to regulate all of our life. This is to be expected, because worship *is* all of life. Everything we do should be done in obedience to God's teachings. Our application of His truth determines the specifics we apply to life and worship in accordance with the general principles of the Bible.

In the light of Jesus' interaction with the Pharisees, the principles that regulate our worship should not be used to enforce traditionalism nor any one style of music in worship. The regulative principle sets us free from human traditions for the worship of God in a manner that honors Him and applies the principles of His teachings. We worship in our local settings and cultural environment that He Himself has created and in which He places us (Acts 17:26). The Scriptures do not have a specific list of appropriate events for our congregational worship. We have to search the Scriptures to determine what is appropriate or inappropriate to do when the local church meets to worship together as a body, in the Name of Jesus Christ.

For example, there is no New Testament command to administer baptism in a Sunday meeting, and there is no historical record of that ever being done in the New Testament period. Baptisms in the New Testament are typically performed outside of formal meetings. But the nature of baptism, as a sign and seal of the covenant of grace, and as a solemn, public oath to the Lord and profession of faith in him, surely makes it appropriate as a part of public Christian worship. First, baptism cannot be other than public. Second, it is administered in the name of Christ, even *into* the name of Christ, and therefore is appropriately performed in a meeting held in Jesus' name. Third, it is the rite of entrance into the church; therefore, it must be witnessed by a gathering of at least some of the leadership of the church.[42]

Elements of Worship from Scripture

1. *Greetings and Benedictions: e.g. Romans 15:33; 1 Corinthians 16:23-24; 2 Corinthians 13:14, 27; that were read in the apostolic letters at public gatherings of Christians.*
2. *Reading of Scripture: 1 Timothy 4:13; 2 Timothy 3:15-17; Nehemiah 8:8.*
3. *Preaching and Teaching: Acts 20:7; Titus 1:9; 2 Timothy 4:2.*
4. *Prayer: Acts 2:42; 1 Timothy 2:1-2.*
5. *Song: 1 Chronicles 16:9; 1 Corinthians 14:26; Ephesians 5:19-20; Colossians 3:16.*
6. *Vows: Psalm 50:14; 65:1, 76:11, in baptism, in reception of new members, in ordination of church officers, and in marriage.*
7. *Confessions of Faith of the group: 1 Kings 8:33-35; 2 Chronicles 6:24-26; 1 Timothy 6:12-13.*

8. *Sacraments: Baptism, The Lord's Supper; 1 Corinthians 11:17-34; Matthew 28:19; Acts 2:38.*
9. *Collections and Offerings: 1 Corinthians 16:1-2.*

Expressions of Fellowship
(i) *Prayers for one Another: Hebrews 10:24-25.*
(ii) *Fellowship with Christ and fellow Christians at the table of The Lord's Supper: Acts 2:42-47.*
(iii) *Greeting one another with a Holy Kiss Romans 16:16; 1 Corinthians 16:20; 1 Thessalonians 5:26; 1 Peter 5:14.*

Holy kisses were perhaps exchanged during worship, just as people shake hands and greet one another in many churches today. The greeting, in God's presence, sets apart the worshipers as members of the body of Christ, declaring their love for one another in Jesus.

The Distinguishing Mark of the Church at Worship
We should remember that love is *the* "mark of the church", that which distinguishes the church from the world (John 13:34-35). Therefore, it is appropriate for us to say and do things in worship to encourage our friendship for one another in the Lord.

For example, some people think that announcements during the service are a distraction from worship. Announcements can often be an annoyance, because of their length, frequency, or inappropriate presentation. It is appropriate, however, in worship to announce opportunities for further teaching, ministry, and general "body life" (including social events). It is entirely proper in worship to give public thanks to people in the congregation, and to God for them, who have in some special way served God and their brothers and sisters in Christ. To avoid any distraction announcements can come before calling one another to worship. Notice how Paul does this in Philippians 1:3-6, 4:10-19, a letter that was doubtless read during worship to the church at Philippi.

There are many specific actions that are also mentioned in Scripture, such as clapping hands (Ps. 47:1), raising hands (Ps. 63:4; 134:2; 1 Tim. 2:8), choir singing and instrumental music (Ex. 15; 1 Chron. 25:1-31; Ps. 150), congregational responses (Deut. 27:14-15; Ps. 118:2-4; 135; 1 Cor. 14:13-17), dance (Ex. 15:20; Jer. 31:4; Ps. 149:3; 150:4), and choosing leaders (Acts 1:12-26). Not all need be practiced and certainly not all in one meeting. It's a matter of practicing wise Christian freedom, carefully observing and conforming to the general principles of Scripture that allows for a variety of godly practices. The elders of the church have the responsibility to determine these practices in the light of Scripture.

The Role of the Preacher
We don't come to worship the preacher. We do come to worship Christ in response to the preaching of his word by the preacher.

The story is told that Thomas K. Beecher once substituted for his famous brother, Henry Ward

Beecher, at the Plymouth Church in Brooklyn, New York. Many curiosity seekers had come to hear the renowned Henry Beecher speak. Therefore, when Thomas Beecher appeared in the pulpit instead, some people got up and started for the doors. Sensing that they were disappointed because he was substituting for his brother, Thomas raised his hand for silence and announced, 'All those who came here this morning to worship Henry Ward Beecher may withdraw from the church; all who came to worship God may remain.' The example of godly leaders is helpful, but only the Savior is worthy of our worship and devotion. Jesus is our Redeemer. We worship God our Father through Christ in the power of the Holy Spirit from the heart.

Music in Worship

Human traditions of particular circumstances common to any activity or society ought not to be set on the same level as Scripture nor imposed upon the church universal (Matt. 15:1-9). Scripture's commands set us free within its general limits to worship God in the language of our time and to apply God's commandments in a way that will build up the people of God in their worship within their contemporary culture.

We know also that we are to communicate God's truth to the present generation through our lives (1 Thess. 1:5-6) and the telling of the story of Jesus. The truth of our experience with Jesus gives meaning to the revealed word of God. The dilemmas of life are faced at the individual level. Jesus the Christ rescues each person from his or her dilemma and the way we worship should communicate this truth of our Redeemer Lord. The presence of God in our midst when we worship should affect even the unbeliever so that the visitor says *"God is really among you!"* (1 Cor. 14:25). The joy of knowing Christ's delivering power from sin and purposelessness is expressed in music and song.

An integral part of communication in worship is music. "Music is not an element of worship but a way of enhancing the elements of worship." According to John Frame, the Scriptures teach that God's people are to speak the truth and also to *sing* the truth.[43] 1 Chronicles 16:9 reads: *"Sing to him, sing praise to him; tell of his wonderful acts."* Colossians 3:16 reads, *"Let the word of Christ dwell in you richly as you teach and admonish one another with all wisdom as you sing psalms, hymns and spiritual songs with gratitude in your hearts to God."*

Biblical faith is a faith that sings. Consider these biblical examples: at least 78 references in the psalms show singing as the natural response of grateful worshipers. On the night of His betrayal, Jesus sang a hymn with his disciples before they went to the Mount of Olives (Matt. 26:30). Paul and Silas sang praises to God while they were stuck in the Philippians' jail (Acts 16:25). One day, with the redeemed in heaven, Christians are going to sing a new song to the One who is worthy of our worship (Rev. 5:9).

There is much more to music in worship than we might be aware. Consider how musical forms make God's word more vivid and aid in the memorization of his words and teaching. It is evident from a study of Scripture that the people of God in ancient Middle Eastern cultures passed on the revelation of God's word in story and song. The most important events were expressed in poetry and music. John Frame writes: "The earliest poetry in Scripture appears at the creation of man in Genesis 1:27. Poetic-musical language also appears at the institution of marriage (Gen. 2:23), the giving of curses and redemptive promises (Gen. 3:14-18), Lamech's prideful and murderous boasts (Gen. 4:23-24), God's covenants with Noah (Gen. 8:22; 9:6,25-27), Abraham (Gen. 12:2-3), and Hagar (Gen. 16:11-12), Isaac's blessing of Jacob (Gen. 27:27-29) and Esau (Gen. 27:39-40), and Jacob's blessing on his sons (Gen. 49). In Exodus, Moses supplements the prose account of Israel's deliverance from Egypt with a song (Ex. 15). Later, God gives to Israel a song, which is to be His witness against them when they break the covenant given through Moses (Deut. 32). Thus begins a long history of redemptive songs conveying God's revelation."[44]

Solomon's "Song of Songs", Mary's "Magnificat" of Luke 1:46-55, and "The Love Song" of 1 Corinthians 13 show that music makes God's revelation more vivid and memorable. As Frame says, "the function of music is to glorify God by investing his word with vividness and memorability that by his grace drives that word into the heart."[45]

Music in worship is a way of employing many biblical principles of worship in the local service: praise (Ps. 8; 145–150), thanksgiving (Ps. 50:14; 100:4), supplication (Ps. 5:1-3), confession of sin (Ps. 51), confession of faith (1 Tim. 3:16), lament (Ps. 6; 10; 137), pronouncement of blessing (Ps. 4:6; 80:3, 7, 19; 86:16), and teaching (Ps. 1; Col. 3:16). Music is not an "element" of worship, distinct from all others; *it is a way of worshiping God from the heart.*

As powerful a tool in worship as music is, it should never replace or supplant the reading and teaching of God's word. Faith comes from the hearing of the word (Rom. 10:17). While the Word of God can be heard through singing, there is something distinct that the Holy Spirit uses when the Scriptures are heard through reading and exposition. Once one has a saving knowledge of God and knows the peace of mind that Christ alone can give the sinner's conscience, the Holy Spirit opens the mouth to sing God's praise. Salvation and praise go together. Hear David's call to sing praises to God in 1 Chronicles 16:23-33:

Sing to the Lord, all the earth;
   proclaim his salvation day after day,
Declare his glory among the nations,
   his marvelous deeds among all peoples.
For great is the Lord and most worthy of praise;
   he is to be feared above all gods.
For all the gods of the nations are idols,
   but the Lord made the heavens.
Splendor and majesty are before him;

> *strength and joy in his dwelling place.*
> *Ascribe to the L*ORD*, O families of nations,*
> *ascribe to the Lord glory and strength,*
> *ascribe to the L*ORD *the glory due his name.*
> *Bring an offering and come before him;*
> *worship the L*ORD *in the splendor of his*
> *holiness.*
> *Tremble before him, all the earth!*
> *The world is firmly established; it cannot be*
> *moved.*
> *Let the heavens rejoice, let the earth be glad;*
> *let them say among the nations,*
> *"The L*ORD *reigns!"*
> *Let the sea resound, and all that is in it;*
> *let the fields be jubilant, and everything in*
> *them!*
> *Then the trees of the forest will sing,*
> *they will sing for joy before the L*ORD*,*
> *for he comes to judge the earth."*

Controversies over the style of music have always been present throughout the history of the church. It will most likely continue until the time when we join with people of every tongue, tribe and nation to sing praises to Jesus Christ (Rev. 5:9-10). There is no indication that this song of redemption will be limited to one musical style. It is possible that there will be simultaneous musical styles that will blend together into a symphony of praise.

Each time the style and substance of music changed it has wrought a negative reaction among the people of God. At the time of the Reformation both Luther and Calvin introduced hymns in the vernacular using local popular tunes. Luther's majestic hymn *'A Might Fortress is Our God'* is set to a popular beer hall tune of his day. The rhythmic tunes to which Louis Bourgeois set the Psalms received the negative response and were called 'Geneva jigs'.

With the advent of popular tunes for hymns introduced at the time of the Reformation, we can trace this development. The Evangelical Awakening of the 1700s saw a great outpouring of new hymns by Charles Wesley, August Toplady, and others. The change here was to emphasize personal experience.

This was not a new thing since the Psalms that were the worship songs of the Old Testament are full of personal experience. Later hymnody of evangelical revivals in the late 19th century also received the same kind of critique. It was only a matter of time before the music of Fanny Crosby, Ira Sankey, Philip Bliss and others were being called the 'good old hymns'.

The youth movements that followed World War II also produced their own style. These were largely popular choruses. The counter-culture of the 1960's in the "Jesus People" movement put great emphasis on scriptural songs sung with guitar in a folk style. We have also seen the rise of Gospel jazz, Gospel music, and Gospel rock.[46]

In Scripture, new acts of God call for "new songs" (Pss. 33:3; 40:3; 144:9; 149:1; Isa. 42:10; Rev. 5:9; 14:3). God delivered his people from Egypt, and they sang a new song (Ex. 15). He gave them water in the wilderness, and they sang (Num. 21:17). He renewed the covenant and committed it to their memory with the song of Deuteronomy 32. The Spirit conceived Christ, and Mary responded with her Magnificat (Luke 1:46-55; compare 1:67-79; 2:14, 29-32). This picture is not one of a static hymnal given by God for all time; rather, it is the dynamic picture of God continually doing wonderful deeds and His people responding to them with shouts of praise. Just as God's deliverances elicit new prayers of thanksgiving and new subject matter for preaching, so they elicit new songs.

We can and do use all kinds of instruments (Pss. 68:24-25; 98:4-6; 149:3; 150:1-6), choirs, ensembles and soloists. 1 Chronicles 15:16 tells us *"David told the leaders of the Levites to appoint their brothers as singers to sing joyful songs, accompanied by musical instruments: lyres, harps and cymbals."* In Psalm 150 David tells us to *"praise God in his sanctuary…with tambourine and dancing."* In Psalm 47 the Sons of Korah tell us to *"clap your hands, all you people groups, shout to God with cries of joy."* In Psalm 63:4 David says, *"I will praise you as long as I live, and in your name I will lift up my hands."* This is music of the body! Clapping expresses joy. Lifting hands is a way of focusing on God as the sole object of worship and sole source of blessing.

When we appreciate music that doesn't immediately appeal to us, it is then that we grow together. It is in the learning of the new ways to praise God that we grow. The goal of history is the gathering of a countless number of Christians from every tribe, tongue, and nation joining in praise to God. One way we learn unity in our time and culture before that Great Day is to learn one another's music and praise God with one united joyful heart.

APPENDIX 1

"Guess Who's Coming to Dinner?"[1]

Behold I stand at the door and knock. If anyone hears my voice and opens the door, I will come in to him and eat with him.

(Rev. 3:20)

This is a time when a number of our young people will be giving their public confession of faith, and coming to join us at the Lord's Supper. In 1967 there was a movie with Spencer Tracy and Katherine Hepburn entitled "Guess Who is Coming To Dinner?" The parents were very liberal-minded and they taught their daughter to think for herself. One day she brought home her fiancé, an African-American medical doctor. You can picture in your mind the surprise of the parents.

God is a God of surprises, and it always amazes us to see who is coming to the Lord's Supper. It is the

Lord who calls his people to himself. There are not many wise or powerful in the group. God chooses the foolish things to confound the wise. I am certain that we can all identify people whom we would not have chosen. However, they are there as a surprise by God, sitting at the table and dining with the Lord.

In the Middle East the meal is far more significant than it is in our culture. It is only a culture like America that could have invented fast food. Why? Because meals are to be eaten so we can get on to the important things. In the Middle East and the East, the meal is the thing. That is where real life comes to expression.

In China, you always consummate a business deal around the meal. The deal is already fashioned, but it needs the official sanction of the meal. In the Bible meals often provide the context. Two passages of scripture were read today (Isa. 55:1-3; Matt. 22:1-11). Both deal with the meal. In Isaiah 55:1-3 the prophet tells us, *"Come everyone who thirsts, come to the water; and he who has no money, come and buy and eat! Come, buy wine and milk without money and without price. Why do you spend your money for that which is not bread and your labor that which does not satisfy? Listen diligently to me, and eat what is good, and delight yourselves in rich food. Incline your ear, and come to me...."*

In Matthew 22:4-10 Jesus tells us a parable about a king who prepares a wedding feast for his son. He sent out his servants with the following instructions. *"Tell those who are invited, 'See, I have prepared my dinner, my oxen and my fat calves have been slaughtered, and everything is ready. Come to the wedding feast.' But they paid no attention and went off, one to his farm, another to his business, while the rest seized his servants, treated them shamefully and killed them. The king was angry and he sent his troops and destroyed those murderers and burned their city. Then he said to his servants, 'The wedding feast is ready, but those invited were not worthy. Go therefore to the main roads and invite to the wedding feast as many as you find.' And those servants went out into the roads and gathered all whom they found, both bad and good. So the wedding hall was filled with guests."*

It was both the good and bad who were invited. The guest list was full of surprises. Those who we would least expect came to the feast. There are no special advantages given to either the good or bad. Many times it is people who come to Christ out of a pagan background that are continually amazed at the grace of God. It takes special work for those who come from a Christian home. It is so easy to take the blessings of Christ for granted and lose the wonder and amazement of being in Christ. Those from a pagan background immediately experience the contrast between the old and the new. Upon reflection of my own pilgrimage with Christ, I am continually amazed at the contrast between my roots and my present life in union with Christ.

The Table is a Place of Honor

In the Middle East the greatest honor to be bestowed on you is to be invited by someone to their home to dine with them. The Lord's Table is a place of honor. In Revelation 3:20 we hear the word of the risen Christ and the invitation he extends to us. *"Behold, I stand at the door and knock. If anyone hears my voice and opens the door, I will come in to him and will eat with him, and he with me."* To be invited to the Lord's Table is to be honored by Christ himself. This is just not an event that delays us getting home for the football games. This is a very special moment because it is a time when Christ is prepared to honor us.

Upon the completion of my seminary training I had a fellowship to study archeology in the Holy Land. One night this friend of ours, an Arabic Christian, arranged for us to visit a Sheik whose home was just outside of Bethlehem. He was the Sheik of the same tribe from which the young man who discovered the Dead Sea Scrolls came. I remember walking into his place. On the right hand the separate room was filled with women. It was the harem of the Sheik. I entered through the door on the left. I sat down with pillows all around on the floor and was served a meal. Do you know what he was doing? He was honoring us. The greatest honor that can be bestowed on you is to be invited to come and dine with a person and his family. When the family invites you in, you are being honored.

Who is at the table is more important than what is on the table. It is the Lord who meets us at the Table.

The Lord is present in the elements. We are honored by him to dine with him. We remember his broken body and shed blood. We are honored because he says of his people, "You are mine" (Isa. 43:1).

Following the Vietnam War our church sponsored a family of refugees. The parents could not speak English so we became surrogate parents to speak to their teachers at school and to assist the family in their studies. Our son became a close friend to their son. When my son's close friend was married in Dayton, Ohio he asked my son to come to be the pig-bearer. It was the tradition that the husband would take to the bride's house, for the bride's parents, a roasted pig on a platter. My son walked through the streets of Dayton, Ohio from the groom's house to the bride's house with a pig. He was honored by being invited into the family to participate in the meal.

When we went to live in Hong Kong, the Tranh family made it a point to have a great feast for us. They wanted to honor us when we were leaving. When we came home they had another meal for us. It was the issue of honor. Today we are having a number of young people make their confession of faith and come to the Table with the whole church. Together we are going to be honored by Christ himself. It is not important what's at the table, but who is at the Table. This is the table of the Lord. It is His presence that makes the difference.

The Table is for the Unworthy

The table is the place for the unworthy; that is what Grace teaches us. We don't come because we have money; we don't come because we deserve to be here. We come because Christ is worthy. The passage in Revelation Chapter 3:20 is an invitation to dining. In Chapter 5:9 we hear a new song. *"Worthy are you to take the scroll and to open its seals, for you were slain and by your blood you ransomed people for God from every tribe and language and people and nation…."* It is Christ who is worthy. We are received because He has invited us. When we hear His call to come to Him, it's not because we are worthy.

We refer to the Lord's Table as a means of Grace. God has ordained that we will receive his grace through the Word of God, prayer, the sacraments and in the fellowship of God's people. The Lord's Table is an experience of grace because it is an invitation to those who are unworthy. We also experience grace by being strengthened to love God and live in a manner well-pleasing to Him. Every good we receive from God is a gift of grace.

The grace we receive does not come automatically by simply eating and drinking. It is not the outward observance which is the means of grace. The grace is an inward grace received by faith. Simply going through the ceremony does not benefit you. You must come to the Table by faith believing you will meet the Lord there. It is through God's grace that we are made worthy of Him.

A Presbyterian pastor friend of mine from

Philadelphia is a Welshman. He loved to tell a story of back in Wales where his father is a pastor. In their church a "lady of the streets" had come and made a profession of faith in Christ. When she came to her first communion she went to my friend's father and said, "I am so unworthy I cannot come to the Table." His response was, "The Table is precisely for people like you. It is for the unworthy."

The Table is a Place of Love

The third thing about the table is that it is a place of love. The church through the ages has referred to the Lord's Table as *The Eucharist*. Eucharist is the Greek word for thanksgiving. At the Table we eat a meal of thanksgiving for the sacrificial love of God in Christ. He came to offer Himself for the sins of His people. We remember with thanksgiving the sacrifice through the symbols of bread and wine. Thanksgiving comes, at least in this church, once a month. We are thankful because though unworthy, Christ has made us worthy to come. In the presence of God we are accepted in the Beloved one, Jesus Christ. We come to the table because of Him.

It is a special kind of love. In 1 John 3:1-2 we see the uniqueness of this love. "See what kind of love the Father has given to us, that we should be called children of God; and so we are. The reason the world does not know us is that it did not know him. Beloved we are God's children now, and what we will be has not yet appeared; but we know that when he appears we shall be like him because we shall see him as he is." Some translations say "behold what special kind of love." In Classical Greek the word translated 'manner' or 'special' referred to a foreigner.

I remember walking down the streets of Jerusalem.. We were looking for St. George's Cathedral.. I had a deep tan and a mustache and could easily pass for a local person. I stopped a gentleman on the street to ask directions. As soon as I spoke he asked where I was from. My accent did not comport with my looks and immediately he knew I was a foreigner. If he were speaking Greek he would have used the word used by John. The love of God is foreign, special and alien. It comes from somewhere else. Whenever we try to describe God's love we at best never do justice in explaining its depth and richness. God's love is a special kind of love, but it is here now.

God chose the bread and the wine as the symbols because we are creatures of our senses. We learn through our five senses: our touch, our taste, our sight, our smell, and our hearing. He has given us elements that we can actually touch and we can actually taste and we can even smell. So when you take the bread this morning, you'll feel it and you hear the words, "This is my body which is broken for you." This morning, squeeze the bread, crush it between your fingers and then remember the words of Isaiah *"…He was crushed for our iniquities…"* (Isa. 53:5). *"Greater love has no one than this: that someone lays down his life for his friends. You are my friends…"* (John 15:13-14).

As you feel the crushed bread realize that the Messiah was crushed for our iniquities, for our sins. As you drink the cup you can sense that it is the blood of Jesus that washes away our sins. The elements are before us to remind us the fullness of God's love for us. They remind us of those great events when Jesus died, was crushed, and His blood was shed for our forgiveness of sins. Our remembrance of His special kind of love is to be a continual act of His people until He returns again.

The Table is a Place of Nourishment

At the table we look beyond the sacrament. We come to the table to feed on Christ. By faith we are spiritually nourished, but that nourishment is not just simply for this morning. At home you eat a meal and are nourished for several hours. As young boys we would stand in front of a mirror and admire our physique and flex our muscles. The purpose of the nourishment of the Lord's Table is quite different. The nourishment we receive is a preaching of the death of Christ until He comes again. If you do not know Christ personally, this is the time to make a confession that you need this kind of life within you. We are nourished by this meal to know what true life is.

There was a philosophy professor who had a large jar filled with golf balls. He asked his class, "is the jar full?" The students said "yes." Then he took some small pebbles and poured them into the jar. He then asked if the jar was now filled. The students respond that it was. Then he took some sand and he poured it into the jar. He again asked the students if the jar was filled. They all said yes. Then he took a couple of cups of coffee and poured them into the jar. He then said to the students the golf balls are the big issues in life. The pebbles are less important. The sand is those little irritants that seem to consume our life. The coffee is the incidental experiences in life. If I had filled this jar full of sand, there would have been no room for the golf balls. If you permit me, the Lord's Table is like a golf ball. It is important because it is here we come and we feed on Christ. We are nourished and strengthened. We receive grace so we can live our lives pleasing to God.

I heard this story from a man and his wife who had just gotten out of the hospital with cancer. They said it really changed the way they looked at life. We need to focus on the things that really matter. When we come to the Lord's Table it really matters. It should change the way we look at life. In the midst of God's people together we feed on Christ; we are honored, we receive grace we do not deserve, we are loved by God, and we are strengthened by God. It's not an incidental sacrament. It's that which God has ordained by which we will grow into the fullness of the measure of the stature of Christ. It is not nourishment for us to just enjoy our new strength. It is a strength that will allow us to serve the only true and living God.

When our children were small we had a bulletin board at the entrance to our home. On it we would put all kinds of school papers, Scripture verses and poems. One of the poems we taught our children went like this.

Those who get and never give,
may last for years, but never live.

Our Welsh pastor in Philadelphia would end the communion service by saying, "Go into the world and love your neighbor as yourself." To him the purpose of the sacrament was to strengthen the people of God so we would fulfill the righteousness of the Law by loving God with all our mind, heart and strength; and love our neighbors as ourselves. The sacrament shows us what it means to love our neighbor by declaring the purpose of Christ's death to them until He returns.

Let me encourage you, even right now, to begin the process of prayer in your life. Examine yourself and ask, "Do I really want to be strengthened by Christ so that I can love Him and serve my neighbor." I encourage you right now to choose at least one person today who you will serve in the name of Christ. Young people think of how you might be able to serve your parents today because of Christ. Adults think about your spouse, your children, and also think about your neighbor. How can we go into the world and love our neighbors as ourselves?

This is a very special moment. It is a moment that is made special not just simply because it is the first communion of those who are publicly professing

Christ. It is a special moment for all of us who have heard the call of Christ. He has knocked at the door and we, who have confessed Christ as Lord and Savior, opened the door and dined with Him. Christ desires to honor, love and strengthen you for His glory alone.

APPENDIX 2

An Example of an Order of Worship Service

Welcome and Announcements

Prelude

Our Worship Begins

Call to Worship:
>**Leader: Let us worship God, who has done great things.**
>*People: We rejoice in our God, who has made a way through the desert of this world.*
>**Leader: Let us worship God, who has caused streams of mercy to flow in the wasteland.**
>*People: We are the people God has formed through Christ; we worship Him, and we rejoice!*
>**Leader: Let us worship God in spirit and in truth.**
>*People: We praise God for the grace that has saved us. Alleluia! We rejoice!*

*We respond in Song:

How Great is Your Love

*No eye has seen, and no ear has heard and no mind
has ever conceived
The glorious things that You have prepared for
everyone who has believed.
You brought us near and
You called us Your own,
And made us joint heirs with Your Son.*

*(Refrain)
How high and how wide
how deep and how long
How sweet and how strong is Your love.
How lavish Your grace
how faithful Your ways
How great is Your love, O Lord.*

*Objects of mercy who should have known wrath, we're
filled with unspeakable joy.
Riches of wisdom, unsearchable wealth, and the
wonder of knowing Your voice
You are our treasure and our great reward
Our hope and our glorious King*

(Refrain)

*Mark Altrogge
1991 Integrity's Praise! Music
Sovereign Grace Praise
(c/o Integrity Music, Inc.)*

I Will Glory in My Redeemer

*I will glory in my Redeemer whose priceless
blood has ransomed me
Mine was the sin that
drove the bitter nails and
hung Him on that judgment tree
I will glory in my Redeemer
who crushed the power of sin and death
My only Savior before the holy Judge,
the Lamb Who is my righteousness
The Lamb Who is my righteousness*

*I will glory in my Redeemer.
My life He bought, my love He owns
I have no longings for another.
I'm satisfied in Him alone
I will glory in my Redeemer.
His faithfulness my standing place
Though foes are mighty and rush up on me.
My feet are firm held by His grace
My feet are firm held by His grace*

*I will glory in my Redeemer,
who carries me on eagle's wings
He crowns my life with loving-kindness.
His triumph song I'll ever sing
I will glory in my Redeemer who waits
for me at gates of gold
And when He calls me it will be paradise,
His face forever to behold
His face forever to behold*

*Steve Cook, Vicki Cook
2001 Sovereign Grace Worship
(Admin. by Integrity's Hosanna! Music)*

*Prayer of Adoration:
We Come to God in Care
for Others and Ourselves

Prayer of Confession: Psalm 130

Psalm 130
Lord from the depths I call to You;
Lord, hear me from on high
And give attention to my voice
When I for mercy cry.

(Refrain)
I wait—my soul waits for the Lord;
my hope is in His word.
I wait—my soul waits for the Lord;
I trust in Him alone.
More than the watchman
waits for the dawn
My soul waits for the Lord.

Lord, in Your presence who can stand,
If You our sins record?
But yet forgiveness is with You,
That we may fear You, Lord. (Refrain)

O Isr'el, put your hope in God,
For mercy is with Him
And full redemption. From their sins
His people He'll redeem. (Refrain)

(Free Church of Scotland 2003)
(psalmody@freechurchofscotlland.org.uk)
Music Arrangement© by Andrew Claassen

Prayers of Intercession

The Ordinance of Covenant Baptism:
A.N.Other
Covenant child of Joe and Mary Other

We Give to God
We give our Tithes and our Offerings:

The Doxology: Trinity Hymnal No. 731

Praise God from whom all blessings flow
Praise Him all creatures here below
Praise Him above you heavenly host
Praise Father, Son and Holy Ghost. Amen.

We greet one another:
"The Grace of the Lord Jesus Christ be with you."
"And also with you."

We Hear and Respond to the Word of the Lord:
Numbers 5:5-10
Leader: This is the Word of the Lord.
People: Thanks be to God.

The Sermon: *"Kingdom Behavior" Luke 19:1-10*

Communion with the Lord with Bread and Wine

*Confessing the Faith of our Fathers:

We Believe

We believe in God the Father,
maker of the universe
And in Christ His Son our Savior
come to us by virgin birth
We believe He died to save us
bore our sins, was crucified
Then from death He rose victorious
ascended to the Father's side

Jesus Lord of all Lord of all.
Jesus Lord of all Lord of all
Jesus Lord of all Lord of all.
Jesus Lord of all Lord of all

We believe He sends His Spirit
on His church with gifts of power
God His word of truth affirming sends
us to the nations now
He will come again in glory;
judge the living and the dead
Every knee shall bow before Him,
then must every tongue confess

Jesus Lord of all Lord of all.
Jesus Lord of all Lord of all
Jesus Lord of all Lord of all.
Jesus Lord of all Lord of all

Graham Kendrick
1986 Thankyou Music
(Admin. by EMI Christian Music Publishing)

Words of Introduction:
1 Corinthians 11:23-32

Prayer of Preparation for partaking of the Bread and Cup

Distribution of the Bread and Cup

Prayer of Thanksgiving

*Praise to Christ our Savior:
> *All Hail the Power of Jesus' Name*
> Trinity Hymnal No. 297

 We Receive God's Promise of Blessing on Us:
2 Corinthians 13:14

Music postlude

APPENDIX 3

Online Resources for Worship Leaders

CCLI – http://www.ccli.com/
The legal and affordable solution to copyright issues surrounding congregational worship services; complete with an enormous inventory of transposable lead sheets, chord charts, vocal/hymn sheets and audio samples.

Great Commission Publications –
http://www.gcp.org/hymns.asp
The place to buy the Trinity Hymnal and Psalter: a collection of ancient and some modern hymns for the reformed church. Also, complete downloadable orchestrations are now available from this site.

Rejoice: *A Collection of Psalms, Hymns, and Spiritual Songs*
The hymnbook of the Presbyterian Church of Australia. ©Presbyterian Church of Australia, GPO Box 100, Sydney, 2001
ISBN# 0 949197 11 4

Sovereign Grace Music
http://www.sovereigngraceministries.org/music/
As stated on their website, "The mission of Sovereign Grace Music is to provide biblically based lyrics for local churches in an effort to exhort others towards praise of our Savior". *Sovereign Grace* comprises of songwriters such as: Bob Kauflin, Mark Altrogge, and Steve and Vikki Cook. They have been able to publish hundreds of songs since in its twenty year existence. It is their aim to produce modern worship songs with a passionate, Cross-centered focus. The site is very useful in that it provides a store for purchasing audio and music files/books, articles about worship, an index of all of their songs, and information on copyright and permission licensing.

Indelible Grace Music
http://igracemusic.com/
A growing collection of modern hymns and hymn arrangements for the church, from an assortment of writers and musicians. The website provides a store to purchase music books and audio files, helpful articles on worship, and even a forum for discussion.

RUF Hymnbook Online

http://www.igracemusic.com/hymnbook/

The online collection of modern hymns and hymn arrangements sung by *Reformed University Fellowship*, a college ministry across America; includes audio samples, lead sheets, chord charts and a growing number of hymn sheets.

Hillsong Church

http://www.hillsong.com/music/

The home of talented and creative songwriters such as Darlene Zschech, Reuben Morgan (reubenmorgan.com), Joel Houston, Marty Sampson, and many more. Always writing and recording new songs for worship, *Hillsong*, youth band *Hillsong United*, and now *Hillsong London*, are an invaluable resource for modern worship arrangements. This website is more of a store than a worship leader's resource. The actual product can be purchased through the website or found at CCLI.

Matt Redman

http://www.mattredman.com/

One of the most influential worship leaders, songwriter, author, and favorite performer at the *Passion* Conference, Matt Redman's website hosts a store, diary, reflections, and helpful links for the worship leader. Again, his music and songs can be bought on the website or at CCLI.

Chris Tomlin

http://www.christomlin.com/

Fellow member of the *Passion* Conference with Matt Redman, Charlie Hall and David Crowder who partner on the label *Sixsteps Record*. Songwriter Chris Tomlin has written many worship songs. Tomlin's site is geared more toward the music fan than the worship leader. His music, blog and other extras can be accessed at his site.

Charlie Hall

http://charliehall.com/

Yet another member of the *Passion* team, Charlie Hall's website is quite helpful in that he provides chord charts, audio files, an extensive journal, and other helpful resources such as links to creative, inspirational, secular music and useful music equipment and effects.

Worship Together

http://www.worshiptogether.com/

This site consists of many great resources for the worship leader; for instance, learning new songs for worship: *New Song Café*, *Free Song*. It also consists of other helpful provisions: Featured Bible Studies, Articles on Worship and Featured Worship Leaders, forums/discussion boards, upcoming events and conferences, and an online store.

Worship Leader Magazine

http://www.worshipleader.com/

A resource that provides interviews with fellow worship leaders, insight into music equipment, an introduction to new music, and a calendar of helpful conferences and events throughout the world for worship leaders. One may subscribe to this magazine, or they can also subscribe to *Song Discovery*, a collection of modern songs for worship to keep the worship leader up to date: http://www. songdiscovery.com/.

The Worship Renewal Network (WRN)

http://groups.yahoo.com/group/wrn_new/

As stated in the group's description, the WRN is "a relational network of pastors and worship and music directors of the Presbyterian Church in America committed to Biblical, Reformed, and gospel-driven worship that glorifies God, transcends style, edifies the church, and evangelizes the unbeliever." This discussion board discusses a wide range of topics that covers the spectrum of worship: style, composition, service planning, mentoring, etc.

APPENDIX 4

Musical Scores for a Selection of Psalms translated in Metre

PSALM 46

Arr. Andrew Claassen

God is our re - fuge and our strength our e - ver pre - sent aid.
2.The na - tions are in di - sa - rray, the king-doms di - sa - ppear.
3.In e - very land through - out the earth he makes all con - flict cease.
4.Be still and know that I am God on earth e - xal - ted high.

And there - fore though the earth gives way we will not be a - fraid.
God speaks and at His migh - ty voice the whole earth melts with___ fear.
He sha - tters bow and spear and shield and brings His reign of___ peace.
And all the na - tions of the world my name will glo - ri - fy.

The LORD Al - migh - ty is with us to

streng - then and sus - tain for Ja - cob's God, our

strong de - fense and for - tress will re - main. main.

Words: Sing Psalms
The Free Church of Scotland
© 2003
psalmody@freechurchofscotland.org.uk

Psalm 110

Words: Sing Psalms
The Free Church of Scotland
© 2003
psalmody@freechurchofscotland.org.uk

Andrew R. Claassen
© 2007

PSALM 121

Arr. Andrew Claassen

lift up my eyes to the hills, where am I to look for my aid? My
foot He will not leave to slide, His watch o-ver you He will keep. The
Lord will keep watch o-ver you, your shade from the heat and the night. The

help comes to me from the Lord, by whom earth and hea-ven were made.
Lord o-ver Is-rael keeps watch and He will not slum-ber or sleep.
sun will not harm you by day, the moon will not harm you by night.

2.Your The Lord will pro-tect__ you, pro-tect__ you from harm. Your

Life He will e - ver de-fend. He'll guard e-very step,__ e-very step__ that you take,__ both

now and for days with-out end.

3.The

Words: Sing Psalms
The Free Church of Scotland
© 2003
psalmody@freechurchofscotland.org.uk

PSALM 130

Words: Sing Psalms
The Free Church of Scotland
© 2003
psalmody@freechurchofscotland.org.uk

You can contact Andrew Claassen at andrew@epchurch.net for futher information

ENDNOTES

[1] Louie Giglio, *The Air I Breathe: I Worship as a way of life* Sisters, OR: Multnomah Publishers, 2003,1

[2] C.S. Lewis in a letter to Mary in *"Letters to an American Lady"* (Eerdmans 1978, pp. 38-39) writes, "And of course the presence of God is not the same as the *sense* of the presence of God. The latter may be due to imagination; the former may be attended with no "sensible consolation". The Father was not really absent from the Son when He said "Why hast thou forsaken me?" You see God Himself, as man, submitted to man's sense of being abandoned. The real parallel on the natural level is one which seems odd for a bachelor to write to a lady, but too illuminating not to be used. The act which engenders a child ought to be, and usually is, attended by pleasure. But it is not the pleasure that produces the child. Where there is pleasure there may be sterility; where there is no pleasure the act may be fertile. And in the spiritual marriage of God and

125

the soul it is the same. It is the actual presence, not the *sensation* of the presence of the Holy Ghost which begets Christ in us. The *sense* of the presence is a super-added gift for which we give thanks when it comes, and that's all about it. …"

[3]Nigel Hopper, *Encounter with God, "Sing Your Life".* Scripture Union, October-December 2005, 81

[4]Karen Moderow, "The essence of worship is recognizing God's presence, and acknowledging Him as God," in *Moody Monthly,* July/August 2002, 25

[5]Hence the title of Robert Webber's book, *Worship is a Verb—Eight Principles for Transforming Worship,* (Hendrickson Publishers, 2000)

[6]*Written in Spirit and Truth,* (Presbyterian and Reformed Publishing, 1996), 3: italics added

[7]WSC, Question 89

[8]William Temple, *The Hope of a New World,* 30; quoted by Donald P. Hustad, *Jubilate: Church Music in the Evangelical Tradition.* Carol Stream, IL: Hope Publishing, 1981.

[9]Psalm 33:1; 34:1; 35:18; 35:28; 51:15; 63:3; 69:30; 100:4; 135:3; 145:2; 147:1; 150:1-6.

[10]The Hebrew singular form is *elah*, which in Arabic is *allah*.

[11]*Acts,* The Bible Speaks Today Series, Inter-Varsity Press, 1990, p 287.

[12]The Hebrew word *adamah* (Adam) is not gender specific. Genesis 5:2 says, *"He created them male and female and blessed them, And when they were created, he called them man (adamah).*

[13]Adapted from the *Anglican Book of Common Prayer.*

[14]James Montgomery Boice, *Foundations of the Christian Faith*, Downers Grove, IL: Inter-Varsity Press, 1986, p271.

[15]*Ibid.,* p. 300

[16]*Ibid*

[17]LORD is the translation of the Hebrew *Yahweh*. When

the lower case Lord is used it is the translation of the Hebrew *Adonai* and reflects the nature of the master-servant relationship. When *Yahweh Adonai* appears it is translated Sovereign LORD.

[18]Warren Wiersbe, *Be Complete: How to Become the Whole Person God intends You to Be,* Wheaton IL: Victor Books, 1981, p. 110.

[19]The Heidelberg Catechism makes the point as follows: Question 31: Why is he called "Christ meaning 'anointed'"? Answer 31: Because he has been ordained by God the Father and had been anointed with the Holy Spirit to be our chief prophet and teacher who perfectly reveals to us the secret counsel and will of God for our deliverance; our only high priest who has set us free by the one sacrifice of his body, and who continually pleads our cause with the Father; and our eternal king who governs us by His Word and Spirit, and who guards us and keeps us in the freedom he has won for us.

The following references help clarify further: Acts 3:22; Deuteronomy 18:15; John 1:18; 15:15; Hebrews 7:17; Psalm 110:4; Hebrews 9:12; 10:11-14; Romans 8:34; Hebrews 9:24; Matthew 21:5; Zechariah 9:9; Matthew 28:18-20; John 10:28; Revelation 12:10-11.

[20]Peterson, *The Message.* Colorado Springs, CO: Navpress, 2002, p. 2036.

[21]See Charles Van Engen, *God's Missionary Church: Rethinking the Purpose of the Local Church.* Grand Rapids, MI: Baker Book House, 1991, p. 69.

[22]Anne Ortlund, *Up with Worship*! Ventura, CA: Regal, 1978.

[23]1 Corinthians 12:12-17; Acts 2:17 (cf. Joel 2:28); 1John 2:27; Matthew 10:32; Romans 10:9-10; Hebrews 13:15; Romans 12:1; 1 Peter 2:5, 9; Galatians 5:16-17; Ephesians 6:11; 1 Timothy 1:18-19; Matthew 25:34; 2 Timothy 2:12.

[24]Westminster Confession of Faith 8:1

[25]Westminster Shorter Catechism, Question 26.

[26]Dorothy Sayers, *"The Man Born to be King."* Grand Rapids, MI: Wm. B. Eerdmans Publishing, 1979.

[27]James Montgomery Boice, *Psalms, Volume III*: Grand Rapids, MI: Baker Book House, pp 898-905

[28]Walter Chantry, *Praises for the King of Kings.* Carlisle, PA: Banner of Truth Trust, 1991, pp 41-82.

[29]See Footnote 17 for the meaning of *Yahweh* and *Adonai.*

[30]Chantry, *Praises for the King of Kings,* Banner, 1991, 59.

[31]*Ibid.*

[32]James Montgomery Boice, *Psalms, Volume III* (Baker, 1998), p. 895

[33]George Matheson, 1841-1906. http://www.hymnsite.com/lyrics/umh421.sht

[34]*Alfred Lord Tennyson's Poetry.* http://www.tennysonpoetry:home

[35]Westminster Shorter Catechism, Q. 98

[36]The New Testament word *homolegeo* in (to confess) means to say the same thing. In confession we say the same thing about our sin that God says about it.

[37]*The Message,* p. 1338.

[38]John Frame, *Worship in the Spirit and Truth.* Nutley, NJ: Presbyterian and Reformed Publishing, 1996, 25 ff.

[39]Westminster Confession of Faith, 21:1

[40]Westminster Confession of Faith, 1:6.

[41]John Frame, *Worship in Spirit and Truth.* Phillipsburg, NJ: Presbyterian and Reformed Publishing, 1996, p. 40.

[42]*Ibid.,* p 55.

[43]*Ibid.,* p. 111.

[44]*Ibid.,* p. 112.

[45]*Ibid.,* p. 14.

[46]This brief history is indebted to John Frame, *Ibid.,* pp 115-120.

Appendix 1

[1] Sermon preached by Dr. Samuel F. Rowen on December 4, 2006 at the Evangelical Presbyterian Church, Cape Coral, Florida.

BIBLIOGRAPHY

An Australian Prayer Book for use together with The Book of Common Prayer, 1662. The Standing Committee of the General Synod of the Church of England in Australia, Sydney, 1978.

Boice, James Montgomery, *Psalms. Vols. 1-3*. Grand Rapids, MI: Baker Book House, 1994.

The Book of Church order: Presbyterian Church in America, Part III, The Directory for the Worship of God. The office of the Stated Clerk of the General Assembly of the Presbyterian Church in America, June 2002.

Common Prayer and Administration of the Sacraments, etc., of the Church of England. The Syndics of the Cambridge University Press.

Dawn, Marva J., *Reach Out without Dumbing Down*. Grand Rapids, MI: Wm. B. Eerdmans Publishing Company, 1995.

Frame, John M., *Worship in Spirit and Truth*, Phillipsburg, NJ: Presbyterian and Reformed Publishing, 1996.

_____., *Contemporary Worship Music: A Biblical Defense*, Phillipsburg, NJ: Presbyterian and Reformed Publishing, 1997.

Giglio, Louie, *The Air I breathe: I worship as a way of life!* Sisters, OR: Multnomah Publishers, 2003.

Johnson, Terry L., (ed.), *Leading in Worship*. The Covenant Foundation, 1996.

"Style and Substance—Is There a Right Way to Worship?" in Moody Monthly, Volume 102 Number 6, July/August 2002.

Navarro, Kevin J., *The Complete Worship Leader*. Baker Books, 2001.

Old, Hughes Oliphant, *Worship That is Reformed According to Scripture, Guides to the Reformed Tradition series*, John H. Leith and John W. Kuykendall, eds.. John Knox Press, 1984.

Ortlund, Anne, *Up With Worship: How to Quit Playing Church*. Broadman and Holman, 1982.

Sing Psalms (New Metrical Versions of the Book of Psalms). Free Church of Scotland, 15 North Bank Street, Edinburgh, EH1 2LS, 2003.

Torrance, James B, *Christ in our Place: the Joy of Worship* in *A Passion for Christ*, Chapter 3, edited by Gerrit Dawson and

Jock Stein. The Handsel Press and PLC Publications, 1999, pages 35 -51.

Van Engen, Charles, *God's Missionary People: Rethinking the Purpose of the Local Church*. Grand Rapids, MI: Baker Book House, 1991.

Webber, Robert E., *Worship is a Verb—Eight Principles for Transforming Worship*. Hendrickson Publishers, 2000.

The Westminster Confession of Faith and Catechisms. Glasgow: Free Presbyterian Publications, 1973.

The Worship Sourcebook. Faith Alive Christian Resources, 2850 Kalamazoo Avenue, S.E., Grand Rapids, MI 49560, and Baker Books, 2004.

Created For Worship

From Genesis to Revelation to You
Noel Due

"This is a gale of fresh spiritual air: it is brilliant."
Rev David Jackman
Cornhill Training Course, London

Created for Worship
From Genesis to Revelation to You
Noel Due

Noel Due has produced a hugely important work into the biblical theme of worship, demonstrating the centrality of worship for human existence. He traces the theology of worship in the Bible and shows its significance for all the people of God. There is a comprehensive analysis of 'Worship' from Genesis to Revelation, investigating captivating areas from worship in the letters of Paul and Peter to Jesus and the transformation of worship.

As Christians we should aspire to worship God with all of our being, and Noel Due reveals to us the intensity of the battle for true worship and sheds invaluable light on the issues informing our understanding of worship.

Dr. Noel Due's work …provides a thorough account, especially, of the worship of the patriarchs and that of the temple era. It does an excellent job of showing how Jesus fulfils Israel's worship. I have on a number of occasions wanted to have a book like this to assign to my seminary students in classes on worship, and I'm very grateful to Dr. Due for meeting that need in an excellent way.

John M. Frame
Prof. of Systematic Theology and Philosophy
Reformed Theological Seminary, Florida

Here, at last is a book about worship which truly honours and uplifts the Lord Jesus Christ as its central theme and object. Moving systematically through the whole of the Scriptures, Dr Due shows how worship provides both the fulfilment of our humanity and the focus of our sinful rebellion. Here is close scholarly observation, blended with sharp, contemporary relevance. It is a treasure-trove of insightful analysis of major themes, central doctrines and even whole or part books of the Bible, as they relate to 'the chief end of man'. This tour de force of Biblical theology is a gale of fresh spiritual air: it is brilliant.

Rev David Jackman
Cornhill Training Course, London

ISBN 9781845500269

Robert I. Vasholz

CALLS TO WORSHIP
A POCKET RESOURCE

Calls to Worship
A Pocket Resource
Robert I Vasholz

In the common practice of Christian churches, across many traditions, a call to worship is typically a few lines of Scripture (or a combination of Scripture texts) expressed at the beginning of a church service. The call to worship exhorts God's people to turn from worldly distractions and to focus hearts, minds and actions on revering him.

If you are involved with leading worship in the church or in the home your next question will be 'Where do I go to find them?' Fortunately, Robert Vasholz has done the legwork for you in this book.

The first section is designed to address specific events common to the Church such as Christmas, Easter, etc. The second section pertains to calls to worship that ask for an audible response from God's people. The third part offers a number of calls to worship from the minister alone. It is my honest desire that this will serve as a proper and dignified way to enhance public corporate worship and to invite God's people to be attentive to the service that follows.

> In the call to worship God calls us to give him praise, but the command is not onerous. It is an invitation to respond to God's revelation of himself and his grace. In offering this invitation God is both host and honoree, and God's people are both invited and compelled by his mercy to give him glory. God gives us the privilege of welcome into his presence that we might reciprocate with the gift of worship. Right perception of this gift exchange encourages the worship leader to speak the call to worship with the warmth of heart and openness of gesture that such an occasion of mutual blessing deserves.
>
> **Rev. Bryan Chapell**
> **President of Covenant Theological Seminary**

ISBN 9781845503383

Robert Vasholz

BENEDICTIONS
A POCKET RESOURCE

Benedictions
A Pocket Resource
Robert I Vasholz

Benedictions, invocations to depart with God's blessings, are a feature of the church - every liturgical structure ends with them. They were a feature of the synagogue in Christ's time – indeed Christ himself uses them when he dismisses his disciples on a new task. The word benediction derives from two Latin words that mean "to speak well of".

Benedictions are pronounced by ministers at the close of worship services as an expression of hope and encouragement to God's people to face whatever their future might hold. This makes them a Biblical norm for the end of worship – something we should consider doing each time we leave God's presence and go out into the world. If you are involved with leading worship in the church or in the home your next question will be 'Where do I go to find them?' Fortunately Robert Vasholz has done the legwork for you. He has collected in this one book the benedictions found in scripture along with some additional scripture enriched blessings for use during worship.

Use them to help Christians have a greater effect on the world.

> Robert Vasholz has collected many of the Bible's benedictions and constructed other scripture-enriched blessings for the use of ministers who lead worship. Indeed all Christians will be "blessed" by reading and praying these wonderful words from God.
>
> **David Calhoun in the introduction**

> ... an attractive resource, which can enlarge the minister's repertoire and be slipped conveniently into his pocket.
>
> **Rt Rev Dr J Barry Schucksmith**
> **Royal Navy (Rtd)**

ISBN 9781845502300

Robert Letham

THROUGH
WESTERN EYES

Eastern Orthodoxy: A Reformed Perspective

Through Western Eyes
Eastern Orthodoxy: A Reformed Perspective
Robert Letham

The culture of the Eastern Church is alien to our experience. Yet the more we familiarize ourselves with the Eastern Church the more we recognize, for all the differences, the family resemblances. The family has been parted for a very long time. But chances have arisen to meet again and get to know one another. In recent years, Eastern Orthodoxy has emerged vividly on the radar of Western Christians – hitherto, it was largely ignored. The separation has been due to the long-term historical disruption caused by differences in language, outlook and theology and eventually by the depredations of Islam. Because of these East and West went their separate ways. As a result, the respective theologies appear at times to inhabit parallel universes. However, this ignorance is changing. Eastern Orthodoxy is increasingly popular in the Anglo-Saxon world. It conveys a sense of mystery, of continuity with the past, of dignified worship at a time when evangelical Protestantism is increasingly cheapened and trivialized. This book examines the history and theology of Orthodoxy from a Reformed perspective. There are clear and significant areas of agreement - a common allegiance to the triune God; the person of Christ; the authority of Scripture and the truth of the gospel. At the same time there are many areas of disagreement, where it seems that Orthodoxy and Protestantism are at odds. However, there are also misunderstandings on both sides, where proponents of either position are not normally dealing accurately with what the other holds to be true. In drawing attention to the agreements and misunderstandings Robert Letham trusts that readers may come to a better understanding of exactly where the real differences lie. We can learn from Orthodoxy – if our assumption is that the most important thing is to grow in our knowledge of Christ.

ISBN 9781845502478

T. M. MOORE

'Think of T.M. Moore's work as high-octane fuel... I pray it will
ignite churches with longing for a true visitation of God in our time.'
John Armstrong

PREPARING YOUR
CHURCH FOR
REVIVAL

Preparing Your Church for Revival
T M Moore

We all long for revival, but we tend to pray for it to come without being completely sure what precisely revival is. This book will be a revitalising aid to those of us who desire revived spiritual life for our churches. T. M. Moore offer practical advice on steps, each with secure scriptural foundations, that we can take to prepare our churches for the sovereign work that is revival. This book is clear that there is no conflict between revival being a work of God and the continued and urgent need for God's people to earnestly pray for its appearance. With practical guides to prayer for revival T. M. Moore realises the need for balance and succeeds in providing a book that will help us to refocus on revival, and will prepare our souls and our churches for the mighty work of a Sovereign and loving God.

> "Think of T. M. Moore's work as high-octane fuel, written by a man who loves the church of Jesus Christ and longs to see her full of his glory once again. I pray his 'fuel' will ignite churches with longing for a true visitation of God in our time."
>
> **John Armstrong**
> **President, Reformation & Revival Ministries, Illinois**

T. M. Moore is a Fellow with the Wilberforce Forum and Pastor of Teaching Ministries at Cedar Springs Presbyterian Church in Knoxville, Tennessee. His essays, reviews, articles and poetry have appeared in a wide range of journals, and he is the author of more than ten books.

ISBN 9781857926989

Christian Focus Publications

publishes books for all ages

Our mission statement –

STAYING FAITHFUL

In dependence upon God we seek to help make His infallible Word, the Bible, relevant. Our aim is to ensure that the Lord Jesus Christ is presented as the only hope to obtain forgiveness of sin, live a useful life and look forward to heaven with Him.

REACHING OUT

Christ's last command requires us to reach out to our world with His gospel. We seek to help fulfil that by publishing books that point people towards Jesus and help them develop a Christ-like maturity. We aim to equip all levels of readers for life, work, ministry and mission.

Books in our adult range are published in three imprints.

Christian Focus contains popular works including biographies, commentaries, basic doctrine and Christian living. Our children's books are also published in this imprint.

Mentor focuses on books written at a level suitable for Bible College and seminary students, pastors, and other serious readers. The imprint includes commentaries, doctrinal studies, examination of current issues and church history.

Christian Heritage contains classic writings from the past.

Christian Focus Publications, Ltd
Geanies House, Fearn,
Ross-shire, IV20 1TW, Scotland, United Kingdom
info@christianfocus.com